EASTBOURNE—SEAVIEW HOTEL

On the Front and in the Front Rank, 50 rooms. Tel.—470. See Hotel Directory front of Bradshaw.

From LONDON to THE SOUTH COAST—Sun━

	1	2	3	4	5	6	7	8	9	10	11	12	13	14	15	16	17	18	19	20
	a.m	a.m	a.m	a.m	a.m	a.m	a.m	a.m	a.m	a.m	a.m	a.m	a.m	a.m	a.m	a.m	a.m	a.m	a.m	p.m
			P		P				P		RB			P		P		P		
VICTORIA ....dep.	..	..	9 25	9 28	9 45	..	..	9 48	10 0	10 3	10 18	..	10*18	10 25	10 28	10 45	10 48	..	11 0	11 3	..
Clapham Junction..... "	..	..		9 33		..	..	9 53				..			10 33		10 53	..	..	..	..
LONDON BRIDGE...dep.	..	9 16	9*16	9*16	9 30	..	9 30	..	..	10 0	..	10 16	10*16	10*16	10 30	10 30	..	..	..	..
New Cross Gate..... "	..	9 21	9*21	9*21	9 35	..	9 35	..	..	10 5	..	10 21	10*21	10*21	10 35	10 35	..	..	..	..
Norwood Junction B "	..	9 30	9*30	9*30	9 44	..	9 44	..	..	10 14	..	10 30	10*30	10*30	10 44	10 44	..	..	..	..
East Croydon..........dep.	..	9 35	9 42	9 46	10 1	..	10 5	..	10 18	10 34	..	10 36	10 42	10 46	11 1	11 5	..	11 18	..	..
Purley...................	..	9 40	..	..	..	..	1011	..	..	..	..	10 41	..	..	11 11					
Coulsdon South.........	..	9 44	..	..	..	..	1014	..	..	..	..	10 45	..	..	11 14					
Merstham...............	..	9 50	..	..	..	..	1020	..	..	..	..	10 51	..	..	11 20					
Redhill 246	..	9 57	..	10 1	..	..	1027	..	..	10 50	..	10 57	..	11 1	11 27					
Earlswood	..	9 59	..	..	..	..	1029	..	..	..	..	10 59	..	..	11 29					
Salfords...............	..	10 3	..	..	..	..	1033	..	..	..	..	11 3	..	..	11 33					
Horley.................	..	10 7	..	..	..	..	1037	..	..	..	..	11 7	..	..	11 37					
Gatwick Airport........	..	1010	..	10 9	..	..	1040	..	..	..	..	11 10	..	11 9	11 40					
Three Bridges (below) 234.	..	1016	..	..	..	..	1043	..	..	11 1	..	11 14	..	..	11 45					
Balcombe	..	1022	..	..	..	..	1050	..	..		..	11 21	..	..	11 51					
Horsted Keynes......dep.	1016	..	..	..	1016	..	..	..	..	..	..	..	..	..						
Ardingly	1020	..	..	..	1020	..	..	..	..	..	..	..	..	..						
Haywards Heath C 239...	1024	1029	1014	1022	10 35	1024	..	1056	..	1052	..	11 28	11 14	11 22	11 32	11 58	..	1152		
Wivelsfield (below).....	..	1033	..	..	..	..	..	11 0	..	..	..	11 32	..	..	12 3					
Burgess Hill...........	..	1036	..	..	..	..	..	11 3	..	..	..	11 35	..	..	12 5					
Hassocks D.............	..	1040	..	..	..	..	..	11 7	..	..	..	11 39	..	..	12 9					
Preston Park...........	..	1049	..	1037	..	..	..	1115	..	..	..	11 47	..	11 37	12 18					
Brighton (below).......arr.	..	1051	..	1040	..	..	..	1118	11 0	11 7	..	11 50	..	11 40	12 21	12 0	12 7			
Haywards Heath ...dep.	..	Stop	..	Stop	10 36	1039	..	Stop	Stop	..	..	Stop	..	Stop	11 33	Stop	Stop	Stop		
Wivelsfield (above).....	..		..			1043	..			..	..		..		11 42		..	..		
Plumpton	..		..			1049	..			..	..		..		11 47		..	..		
Cooksbridge............	..		..			1054	..			..	..		..		11 47		..	..		
Lewes 239............arr.	..		..		10 53	1059	..			..	..		a.m		11 53		..	..		
Brighton..............dep.	..	..	..	..	..	1046	..	..	..	..	..	11 14	..	..	..	..	..	..	..	1214
London Road (Brighton)..	..	..	..	..	..	1048	..	..	..	..	..	11 16	..	..	..	..	..	..	..	1216
Falmer.................	..	..	..	..	..	1053	..	..	..	..	..	11 20	..	..	..	..	..	..	..	1220
Lewes..............arr.	..	..	..	..	..	11 0	..	..	..	..	..	11 28	..	..	..	..	..	..	..	1228
Lewes..............dep.	..	..	..	..	..	11 4	11 4	..	..	..	..	..	..	..	12 4	..	..	..	..	..
Southease and Rodmell..	..	..	..	..	..	11 9	11 9	..	..	..	..	..	..	..	12 9	..	..	..	..	..
Newhaven Town ...[Halt	..	..	..	..	..	1114	1114	..	..	..	..	..	..	..	12 14	..	..	..	..	..
" Harbour..	..	..	..	..	..	1115	1115	..	..	..	..	..	..	..	12 15	..	..	..	..	..
Bishopstone............	..	..	..	..	..	1120	1120	..	..	..	..	..	..	..	12 20	..	..	..	..	..
Seaford..............arr.	..	..	..	..	..	1122	1122	..	..	..	..	..	..	..	12 22	..	..	..	..	..
Lewes..............dep.	..	..	..	..	10 54	11 1	Stop	..	..	..	..	11 29	..	..	11 54	..	..	..	..	1229
Glynde.................	..	..	..	..	..	11 6		..	..	..	..	11 34	..	..	..	..	..	..	..	1234
Berwick................	..	..	..	..	..	1112	a.m	..	..	..	..	11 40	..	..	..	..	..	..	..	1240
Polegate 239...........	..	..	..	..	..	1119	1138	..	..	..	..	11 47	..	..	..	p.m	..	p.m	..	1247
Hampden Park F........	..	..	..	..	..	1122	..	..	..	..	1145	11 50	..	..	12 15	..	1245	..	1250	
Eastbourne..........{arr.	..	..	..	..	11 13	1119	1126	1146	..	..	1149	11 54	..	..	12 13	12 19	..	1249	..	1254
{dep.	..	..	..	..	11 17	1129	Stop	Stop	..	..	Stop	11 57	..	..	12 17	..	Stop	..	Stop	125━
Hampden Park F........	..	..	..	..	Stop	1132			..	..		12 0	..	..	Stop	..	..	..	..	1 ━
Pevensey and Westham....	..	..	..	..		1139			..	..		12 7	..	..		..	..	..	..	1 ━
Pevensey Bay Halt......	..	..	..	..		1141			..	..		12 9	..	..		..	..	..	..	1 1━
Norman's Bay Halt......	..	..	..	..		1144			..	..		12 12	..	..		..	..	..	..	1 1━
Cooden Beach...........	..	..	..	..					..	..		12 16	..	..	12 30	..	..	..	..	1 1━
Collington Halt........	..	..	..	..					..	..		12 19	..	..		..	..	..	..	1 1━
Bexhill (Central) G....	..	..	..	..					..	..		12 22	..	..	12 35	..	..	..	..	1 ━
St. Leonards (W.M.).....	..	..	..	..					..	..		12 26	..	..		..	..	..	..	1 ━
" (W.S.).....	..	..	..	..					..	..		12 29	..	..	12 42	..	..	..	..	1 ━
Hastings 56, 59........	..	..	..	..					..	..		12 31	..	..	12 44	..	..	..	..	1 ━
Ore...................arr.	..	..	..	..					..	..		12 34	..	..	12 48	..	a.m	..		

Through Train, Victoria to Littlehampton.
Through Train, Victoria to Bognor Regis.
Runs until 21st September only.
Through Train, Victoria to Littlehampton.

903━ D0409382

In memory of Arthur and Bessy Ashley

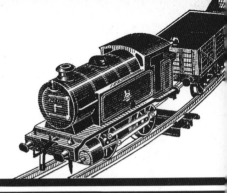

more from

UNMITIGATED ENGLAND

Peter Ashley

Adelphi
Publishers

This edition © Adelphi Publishers 2007
Text © Peter Ashley 2007
Images © Peter Ashley
unless otherwise stated

First published in 2007
By Adelphi Publishers
Northburgh House
10 Northburgh Street
London EC1V 0AT

Text by Peter Ashley
Design by Anikst Design LTD
and Peter Ashley
Edited by Sarah Peacock

ISBN: 978 184159 274 9

Printed and bound in Germany by GGP Media GmbH,
Pössneck

Sales information:
Random House UK
Tel. 020 7840 8463

Orders to:
Grantham Book Services
Tel. 01476 541 000

All rights reserved. No part of this publication may be
reproduced, stored in a retrieval system or transmitted, in
any form or by any means, electronic, mechanical,
photocopying, recording or otherwise, without the prior
written permission of the copyright owners.

10 9 8 7 6 5 4 3 2 1

Frontispiece

In *The Lion and the Unicorn* George Orwell reckoned that
England 'is somehow bound up with solid breakfasts and
gloomy Sundays… ' Well, here's an English breakfast.
It was taken on a Sunday morning, but happily a sunny
autumnal example

Endpapers

The endpapers are taken from the Southern Railway
summer timetables for 1947

LONDON BOROUGH OF WANDSWORTH	
9030 00000 7030 4	
Askews	24-Dec-2009
942 ASHL	£18.99
	WWX0005785/0004

CONTENTS

PREFACE

By Jonathan Meades

Acknowledged and Unacknowledged Masterpieces:

below
Castle Howard in North Yorkshire

opposite
Wartime corrugated-iron barns on the Gartree Road near Stonton Wyville in Leicestershire

Like, say, pastiche, nostalgia has become a dirty word. This is hardly surprising in a country that is publicly neophiliac, restlessly progressive, obsessed by perpetual change, riddled with exciting initiatives. Yet privately nostalgia is an affect that all but the most brute sensibilities entertain. Without nostalgia – literally, the yearning for a lost home – the canon would be vastly diminished. No Proust, no Chateaubriand, no Housman, no Hopkins. If we are true to ourselves we have to admit that in our imaginative longing we persistently turn back the clock, we recurrently 'tompeep down the hedges of the years'. (Nor would there be Nabokov.)

Peter Ashley is a man of multitudinous madeleines. He is the gatekeeper to several generations' memories. Anyone who had the good fortune to be alive in the England of the 1950s will discover in his work endless triggers which bring back that far from grim, far from grey decade. The received ideas are wrong. It was, actually, a time of multi-coloured content. This is not to say he makes us wish to crack open a bottle of Bovril or a tin of Bird's Custard Powder. It is the sight of their packaging and jolly advertisements rather than the dubious taste of their contents which are such potent keys to mnemonic bliss. And one memory lights another with synaesthesiac ease. The Spratt's calligram smells of seed and sacks.

The douce past is not however just within our brain waiting to be released. It is on celluloid – which is probably the best place for the nightmare called Meccano that plays such a central part in Tim Preece's *The Combination*, which Peter Ashley properly adjudges superb.

It is in the increasingly overpriced Rupert Bear annuals – which inevitably make me think of the former Rosicrucian church in Nutwood Street near Peckham Rye Common.

It is, most of all, in the overlooked and often bedraggled buildings which have miraculously survived the depredations of vandal councils and oik developers. Prefabs, Nissen huts, sheds built of corrugated iron which was once the material of the future, wonky cricket pavilions, deserted lodges, bedraggled shack colonies, beached boats, lean-tos, rolling stock that rolled its last long before Sir Nigel Gresley designed the A4 Pacific. Peter Ashley is our foremost chronicler of these structures. His is an earnest endeavour for they are constantly at risk, they receive no statutory protection and are worth less than the land they stand on. He values them and encourages us to value them.

The atypical – Broadway, Finchingfield, a Vanbrugh palace, a Pugin church – is seldom any longer in danger; we learnt a lesson the hard way, we rue the depredations of the post-war years. But it is the everyday and the humble which evidently constitute the most vital part of England's texture, which lend it the flavour it still possesses if we bother to look and decline to feast our eyes on a diet of acknowledged masterpieces. This book is, amongst much else, a hymn to unacknowledged masterpieces, to the quiet genius of the bodger, the bricoleur and the adept of the Birmingham screwdriver.

INTRODUCTION

above
An MG Midget Series
'TD'. The brochure,
c. 1952, proudly states
that the car 'Goes like a
flash… grips the road like
a *limpet*'

We approach the *Unmitigated* town of Market Pigborough by a main road that runs round a barrow-like hill known to the locals as Pig's Snout. At the summit is a three-sided folly tower, where a boy and a girl (he wears National Health spectacles and she has her hair in blue ribbons) sit watching us with their chins on their knees. They see our MG TD sports car passing in and out of the trees and then their attention is distracted by a shrill whistle cutting through the morning air. The boy nudges the girl and points down the other side of the hill to where a black tank engine runs backwards, pulling a rake of teak coaches over silver bright rails. The line of track is marked by telegraph poles, curving round to where our road is barred by white level crossing gates surmounted by red oil lamps. A signalman is ascending the steps of his weatherboarded box,

wiping his hands on a square of cotton waste as the urgent sound of a bell rings from the interior. He gives us a polite acknowledgement as the train shuffles past, wisps of steam rising up from its cylinders as the sleepers laid down over the crossing move gently up and down. As the gates are opened we look to the right and see a handful of passengers gathering under a station platform awning to give their tickets to the collector. A tall youth in grey flannel trousers and a sports coat is given help by a porter to get his racing bike out of the guard's van. He temporarily props it up against a parcels trolley as he puts his bicycle clips on. Craning our necks a little we also see a green single-decker bus pulled up in the station yard next to a Royal Mail van, its indicator blind showing a succession of local outlying villages. We pass a coal yard with its smoking office chimney and sign in the window saying 'Coalite'; a timber yard with planks being loaded onto a flatbed railway truck; and then a cast-iron sign with its colourful coat of arms welcoming us to the town.

On the left we see a garage with two petrol pumps outside. Both have long red rubber delivery hoses that enable the proprietor – when he comes out from under the battleship-

Ransomes

grey Austin Devon he's mending – to swing them out over cars to put fuel into far side tanks. The petrol is BP, and the sign is a striking no-nonsense green shield with yellow letters. Over the road is a pub, The Pig in The Poke, with the local brewery name on a ceramic sign by the door. Windows with sandblasted glass say 'Saloon' and 'Snug'. If we had the time to pop in later we'd find a gloriously unhealthy fug building up from the blue wreaths of cigarette smoke rising up to the nicotine-stained ceiling. The iron-legged wooden tables will soon have place settings of straight-sided half-full glasses and open Woodbine packets.

Our road widens out into the market square where we park the MG under the shade of a big chestnut tree. On one side is The Blue Boar Hotel, the name picked out in cut-out gold letters on the orange brickwork. The sound of a hoover comes from an open upstairs sash window and a white-haired old man in a green apron is polishing the brass menu holder next to the door. He looks up and says, 'Good morning,' to a lady passing by with a basket on little wheels, touching a metaphorical hat with his index finger. Opposite the hotel we see three shops – a greengrocer's with pyramids of fruit and vegetables, a bakery with the smell of fresh loaves

and glass dishes displaying buns in the window, and an ironmonger that looks as if most of the big items of stock are out on the pavement. The proprietor of the latter is loading up the back of his blue Bedford van with two galvanised dustbins, a roll of wire netting and an Aladdin greenhouse heater. His assistant is scratching his head and staring at a Ransomes lawnmower that's been lifted out of a shooting brake by a colonel in tweeds, but he finds a second or two to wink at the girl serving in the teashop on the corner, who blushes as she takes an order from the local solicitor. There are two or three solicitors' offices in Market Pigborough, lined up in a Georgian brick terrace on a narrow cul-de-sac that leads off the square up to the stone-built church (Norman nave, Perpendicular tower with a St George's flag) and the extensive graveyard under dark spreading yews.

above
A Ransomes motor mower, yours for £54 18s 3d. In 1959

right
Fruit and veg on the high street. Romsey, Hampshire

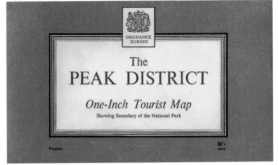

above left
Flowers in the church.
Lower Benefield,
Northamptonshire

above right
Ordnance Survey Tourist
Map, 1963

As we walk up the path from the lychgate, the verger scurries past with a 'Lovely morning', his black cloak floating out behind him like a billowing sail in the breeze. Inside, the church has not been over-restored by the Victorians, but they did get in some oak pews that still succeed in looking right. A long row of red hymnbooks – Ancient & Modern – stretch out along a shelf of the pew nearest the door, contrasting with the blue prayer books in a bookcase on which lies the visitors' book. The latest entry reads, 'What a perfect surprise,' followed by an address in Huntingdonshire. The red pencil for comments is attached to the book with a length of yellowing string. Two ladies arranging flowers around the double-decker pulpit murmur a greeting as they cut gladioli stems down to size. Meanwhile a few trial notes peep out from the organ loft, the organist adjusting his feet for the pedals as if to drive off in a new car.

The church clock strikes eleven and we make our way back up to the square. On this approach we enter past the war memorial, where the cyclist from the station is munching an apple from the greengrocer's as he studies his Ordnance Survey map spread out on the steps. In front of us now is the post office, a neo-Georgian affair perfectly suited to the town. A red postman's bike with white mudguards is propped up against the wall. From inside we can hear the rhythmic tattoo of official rubber stamps accompanying the buying of postal orders and the sending of telegrams. As we stand listening, a Morris GPO (General Post Office) telephone van comes out from a yard at the side of the post office. It is in a beautiful shade of dark green with a Royal cipher on the side and a wooden ladder strapped down to the roof.

We must move on, so we go into the grocer's next to the post office to find something for our lunch. The proprietor is outside in a white

top right

The crown used by the GPO on their mid bronze-green telephone vehicles

bottom right

On the beach. The latest fashionable swimwear from Robinson & Cleaver of Regent Street. Around five hundred points for each item in the Kensitas gift catalogue

all away in a wicker basket that we stuff between us in the MG, together with a couple of bottles of Red Snout Ale, the last cottage loaf from the baker's and a last-minute addition of fresh green apples from the orchard on Folly Lane.

As we cross over the River Pygge on the narrow medieval bridge we look downstream to see a wharf with one Meccano-like crane lifting concrete sewer pipes (made down the road at Pigborough Mills) into the bowels of a freighter moored up at a corn-strewn wharf. On this side of town there is suddenly the smell of the sea, just five miles away, and we decide to indulge ourselves with a picnic on the beach at Seapig Sands. Just as we pass the Victorian Hadsomes Brewery, with its high water tower, we hear the sound of the lunchtime hooter calling the workers to the canteen. A little later, as the last rows of terraced cottages diminish behind us, we see the GPO van pulled up on a grass verge as its driver – strapped on with a leather belt to a creosoted telegraph pole – renews a telephone wire. As he snips and twists the copper wire around the ceramic insulators he watches our little car wind through the hedgerows and fields ripe with corn towards the bright line that is the sea.

overall, ticking off a boy who is pumping up the rear tyre of the grocery bicycle that has the grocer's name in a flowing script on a side panel beneath the crossbar. We assemble a picnic made up from ham sliced on a big red Berkel machine and a large section of local cheese cut with a wire on a white porcelain slab. We stow it

There are obviously many ways one can read what I've written so far. A whimsical narration of a bygone age where tea shoppes mysteriously gained an extra 'p' and an 'e'? With the sun always shining? Perhaps a wooden barrel full to the brim with sweet-smelling roseate nostalgia, and no additives to frighten the horses? Well, it could be all those things. But perhaps you've read it with an increasing sense of unease. Let's take a quick look at Market Pigborough last week.

right
One of the last vestiges of a characterful railway clings on in wood and iron at Combe Junction, Cornwall

At a recent town council meeting they tried to pass a motion that would remove the 'Market' from Market Pigborough because, they say, there's no cattle market anymore, and you can't really count the farmer's market that's held in the square every month. The folly has mobile phone masts sprouting out of the top of it and no children climb up to it because they're not allowed out to play anymore. The railway line still runs round the hill, but now it's a single coach train that's painted to look like a budget airliner that pulls up at the station. No one collects tickets; that business has been sorted out on the train by Revenue Protection Officers loaded down with digital surveillance equipment. The station buildings are shared by a beauty parlour (Nails by Raquel) and a firm selling timeshare apartments. There's no signalman and the level crossing is now a continental-style barrier. Both signals and crossing are operated from a darkened room 20 miles away. There is no accommodation for cycles on the train and no porters to help passengers. The bus, looking like a dirtier version of one of those coaches that ferry you about from airport car parks, only goes from the square and doesn't coordinate with train times anyway. Both timber yard and coal yard have

above and opposite
The metamorphosis
of BP from stern but
dependable protector
(1931–2001) to 'Helios',
a smiling friend giving
out leaflets in the green
ecology tent. Trademark
mythology has it that the
original colours were
chosen after a senior
management lunch
in 1930s' Paris, which
consisted of green
asparagus and yellow
Chablis

gone, built over by tightly packed houses with no chimneys and tiny gardens on roads now called Timber's Yard and – not quite brave enough – Collier's Lane. The Market Pigborough sign welcomes us with an additional 'Working for U' and 'Twinned with Oranjeboom'.

The garage has closed (it's a wine bar called The Garage), so we buy petrol and Lattice Pork and Pickle Slices from a 'services' on the bypass where the BP shield has been replaced by a flower drawn with one of those Spirograph things, because BP now means 'Beyond Petroleum'. The pub opposite is still there but it's now called The Pig in Trousers and has a big plastic banner across the front that says 'Steak and Chips and a pint for a fiver every nite'. Many of the locals stay at home since their fags are stubbed out by the council and they can't talk to each other because they can't hear anything over the football continually playing on the SupaWide screen above their heads.

Most of the chestnut trees in the square were cut down when it was pointed out that a stray branch falling could result in a damaging insurance claim. The Blue Boar Hotel is now part of a chain called Best English Hotels and the management changes every three months. The pyramids of fruit and veg are still piled up at the greengrocer's, but the produce is all trucked in from Serbia. The bakery and ironmonger have gone, replaced by two rival estate agents. The blushing girl now runs the teashop; she married her lawnmower boy who these days looks after gardening equipment at the local Do-It-More, also on the bypass.

The lady vicar scurries purposefully under the churchyard yews. Did she make the decision about the pews or was it her predecessor? Anyway, they've gone. Replaced by individual upholstered chairs that look like a job lot from a 1970s' public library. Arranged in a semi-circle round a new 'more companionable, don't you think?' altar covered with an abstract tapestry called 'Our Lord Comes To Market Pigborough'. The hymn and prayer books have also gone; now it's a pile of booklets called *Hallelujah! It's Sunday!*. The organ's still there but the chancel steps have a worrying row of guitar stands placed on them. Nobody writes Huntingdonshire much in the visitors' book these days.

The war memorial still sees white-haired veterans gathering at the steps with their poppy wreaths every November, despite the strident tones of a journalist who said it should stop because 'it all happened a long time ago and what relevance has it these days anyway?'.

above
Keeping faith, lest we forget. The war memorial at Thorpe Achurch in Northamptonshire

opposite
Keeping faith, the hollyhock. An annual dazzling display to lift the spirits in English cottage gardens

The post office is another wine bar called The Post Office and what's left of the real post office is now incorporated into the back of the little supermarket and newsagent's next door, which used to be the grocer's. (Bestco saw off the grocer and his grocer's bike many years ago. They're down on the bypass too.) The post office counter is well patronised, mainly because half of the village post offices surrounding Market Pigborough were closed. So there's always a frightful queue, mainly composed of the town's elderly, confused by the flashing number that treats them as if they're waiting their turn at Bestco's delicatessen counter.

The picnic we ordered online from Fortnum's is sitting in its wicker basket in the back of our new Ssangyong 4x4. As we go over the medieval bridge we see that the wharf buildings are in scaffolding, with a huge developer's hoarding that says 'Luxury Loft Living Apartments. Single bedroom starter homes from just £300,000.' Concrete sewer pipes are still made down at Pigborough Mills, but they're now forklifted onto articulated lorries that continually wedge themselves against the parapets of the bridge. We are very pleased we can still get Red Snout in bottles from the Hadsomes new brewery shop, but we

exchange glances and raise our eyebrows when we pass a white BT van on the grass verge that reads 'openreach' on the side. We start to say something about how it was all somehow so much better than this, but we stop and just stare out over the open fields in silence.

❧

The look of England has changed dramatically over the last decade. So many things that we treasured or took for granted in our daily lives have changed irrevocably. But however much I am given to wearing my metaphorical goggles, which filter out the worst excrescences I witness on my travels, England still has enormous capacity to delight our eyes in countless ways. And so although this, and its predecessor, is a picture book of a country lost, it is of course also an appreciation of much that can still be found, if only we can take to heart poet W.H. Davies's lines, 'What is this life if, full of care / We have no time to stand and stare?'.

A GOOD BOOK AND A MUG OF COCOA

Long after the novels and romances of adult life have faded and been forgotten,
the simple stories and tales we read in childhood live on in our hearts.
The Collector's Book of Children's Books, Eric Quayle

opposite
Fireside fun. Detail from
the cover of the 1948
Chicks' Own Annual

There is nothing quite as comforting as a good book, particularly in the halcyon days of childhood. I was very fortunate to be born into a household where books were as common as the bread and dripping we appeared to live on, and lying in front of a roaring fire on rain-soaked mornings with a favourite book was my idea of heaven. That was, until my mother came in and said, 'Shift yourself,' because she wanted to run the Ewbank over the carpet.

The very first book I remember looking at was a nursery rhyme rag book that had a picture of a rabbit walking by a signpost that had 'Norwich' on it. Much later my elder brother told me it was pronounced to rhyme with 'porridge'. My staple diet was of course Enid Blyton; first Noddy, with the iconic illustrations by 'Beek', and then the graduation to The Secret Seven. (I used to imagine I was one of them, but never knowing who the other six were). The Famous Five were always slightly suspect for me – big-shorted Julian bossing everybody about, meek Anne, and I never really got my head round the fact that there was a girl who looked disturbingly like my cousin Molly but was called George. Far better for me was Blyton's alternative gang, the characters that

peopled the book that I serially read – *The Rockingdown Mystery*. This book gave me the idea of breaking and entering deserted and wrecked old houses, a taste for which I still steadfastly maintain.

Once a week I would accompany my mother to the local library, with the promise that if I was good I would be taken a little further to see steam trains shuffling about their business. The library was the converted stable of a big house that had become council offices where we got free orange juice and cod liver oil, and the big black door that opened onto a world of pale wooden counters and shelves always had the latest road safety poster pinned to it (one depicted a motorbike overtaking a lorry on a blind summit with the legend 'Journey's End'. I had nightmares for a week). But I loved the library, with the silence that was only broken by low murmurs and the thump of the date stamp, and the such inviting low shelves of the children's section.

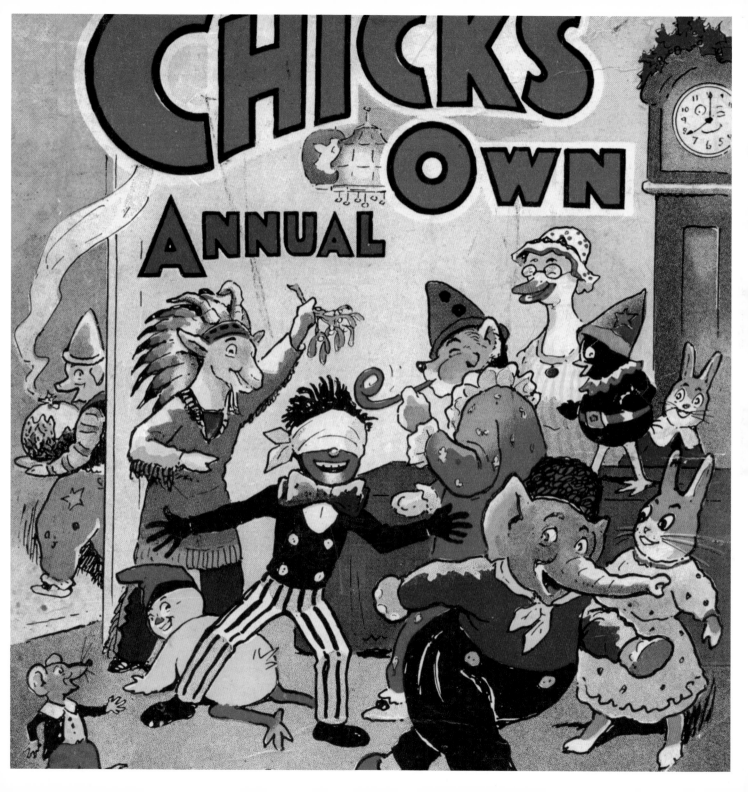

Spine-Tingling Books

above and top right
Books that really made
their colourful presence
felt on children's
bookshelves

bottom right
RMS *Mauretania* steams
purposefully across stiff
covers, and a Turkish
attempt to board a ship is
repelled with just a well-
aimed fist. By Jove

Bookshelves in the early twentieth century were unequivocally colourful places. Here could be found the original dangerous books for boys: tales of courageous derring-do, of doing the right thing – usually dispatching tigers or a swarthy Son of Satan – in remote outposts of the Empire. Books that carried on their spines ranks of Napoleonic soldiers, medieval bowmen and pea-jacketed naval officers. Author G.A. Henty couldn't stop himself, churning out title after daring title, each one eagerly snapped up by well-off boys to read in their town house bedrooms or country house orchards.

The appeal now is more likely to be in their bright pictorial covers rather than in lascar sailors being sorted out with service revolvers, but the non-fiction element can be truly enlightening. Reading about the *Titanic* before it met with the iceberg in *Every Boy's Book of Railways & Steamships*; learning how to put a piano together in *How it is Made*. There were of course books in these bright liveries for all children, and I suspect quite a few girls spirited their brothers' books away to the conservatory.

THE DANDY BOOK FOR CHILDREN

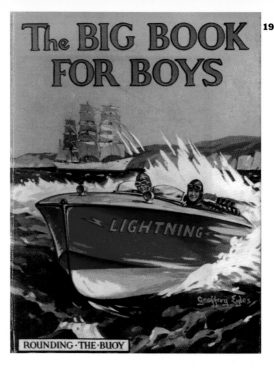

The BIG BOOK FOR BOYS

LIGHTNING

ROUNDING · THE · BUOY

above

Motor boats figuring
large on the covers for
1930s' reward books. How
difficult would it be to use
a lasso effectively whilst
standing up in one?

below

The Girls Budget, c. 1938

THE *Girls' Budget*

Reward Books

I was never really a prizewinner. I think I once got
something for a scurrilous article I put in the
school magazine, and a couple of books for good
attendance at a Sunday School my father frog-
marched me into. Books like *The Cruise of the
Clipper* by Morgan Derham in which adolescent
youths discovered God and good sailing practice
amidst the reedy reaches of the Norfolk Broads.

Thirty years previously, reward books had
been big business. Sunday Schools, and indeed
everyday schools, were often strapped for cash
and publishers, particularly the Oxford
University Press, produced books specifically to
be prizes. They looked amazing with their bold
covers that used words like 'Big' and 'Bumper',
but the colourful cardboard all too often hid
thick, poor quality paper that soaked up the black
ink of the type. Even though there might have
been a coloured frontispiece, the whole effect was
to give a halo of perceived value for money;
cheaply produced books given a Sunday suit of
clothes to make a big impression in crowded
school halls. But sly economics didn't enter
children's heads. Many of these books survive in
good condition because they were treasured and,
quite rightly, appreciated simply for what they
meant in terms of recognition of effort.

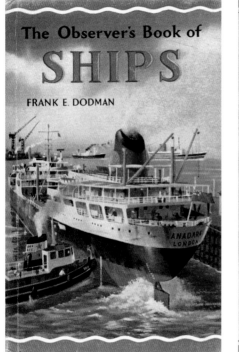

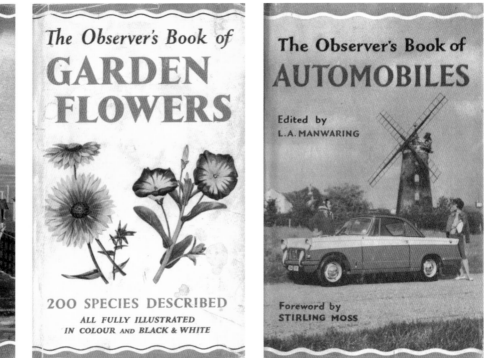

Observer's Books

above

Observer's Books, with the early distinctive 'scallop edge' borders to the covers

The first Observer's Book I ever saw was *Birds*. It didn't have the glorious full-colour jacket with the male and female robins, and there was an inky fingerprint on the front cover. But it was in continual use, desperately thumbed through to identify birds that momentarily flitted into the garden from the 243 species illustrated in those wonderful colour cameos, many by Archibald Thorburn. I would frighten myself by looking at the Long-eared Owl on page 114, hoping I'd never be confronted by it round by the coal shed. But I was soon distracted by *The Observer's Books of Automobiles* which was reissued in a revised and updated edition each year, getting very excited when one year the cover showed the new Triumph Herald Coupé posed in front of a windmill.

These compact pocket books were published by Frederick Warne, whose name appeared on them until 1982. Frederick himself never saw the series, but he was in the forefront of producing 'healthy literature at popular prices'. In his time Warne published the Wayside and Woodland books, many written by nature writer Edward Step. Much of his work was recycled into the Observer's Books, the first

above
A series that pre-dated the Observer's Books, this title was edited in 1941 by Enid Blyton

above right
Immediately recognisable Observer's book covers, using both full colour and simple line drawings

of which, *British Birds* and *British Wild Flowers* appeared in 1937. A forerunner to the *Birds* volume was *Birds of The Wayside and Woodland*, it was edited in 1941 by none other than a young Enid Blyton. But as this soon-to-be-prolific author became immersed in Secret Sevens and Famous Fives, the Observer's series expanded into a hundred volumes with sales of thirty million. Perfectly formed books that introduced generations of children, and grown-ups, to everything from the minutiae of *British Grasses, Sedges & Rushes* to the infinite expanses of *Astronomy*.

Ardizzone Puffins

Opposite

Detail from the cover of
The Otterbury Incident
by C. Day Lewis

above

Edward Ardizzone covers
for Puffin Books

bottom right

Self-portrait of the artist,
1952

Edward Ardizzone was born in 1900; Puffin Books in 1941. Many will know of his illustrations for the *Radio Times*, H.E. Bates's *My Uncle Silas* stories and for his own tales, which started with *Little Tim and the Brave Sea Captain* in 1936. But most of us were probably introduced to his work by Puffin Books, with line drawings scattered about the text, and covers that always incorporated his own distinctive lettering, even on the spines.

There is something uniquely comforting about Ardizzone's drawings. For me they immediately evoke another world; not a fantasia but a hidden, quieter, perhaps more mysterious place. The literary equivalent would be Walter de la Mare's poems for children – Ardizzone illustrated *Peacock Pie* whilst on leave in Cairo in 1945 –, but the authors with whom he is most likely to be associated are Eleanor Farjeon and James Reeves. Look at the front cover of Farjeon's book here. Why is the little girl turned away from the other children? We need to start reading to find out about the eternally skipping Elsie Piddick, which, of course, is exactly what cover design is all about.

Ardizzone's style is deceptively simple. He is quoted in printer W.S. Cowell's *A Handbook of Type and Illustration*: 'Stage 1. The drawing is indicated rather hesitatingly in outline. Stage 2. Shadows are then suggested by a very deliberate even hatching… Stage 3. The shadows are heightened and colour indicated by cross hatching…' If one needed to sum up his style in a couple of words, that 'rather hesitatingly' would do the trick.

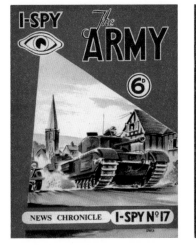

above
Tribal marking

right
A selection of 1950s' I-Spy books. *Wild Fruits and Fungi* was one of a small series that had coloured illustrations on thicker paper and therefore the heftier price tag of one shilling

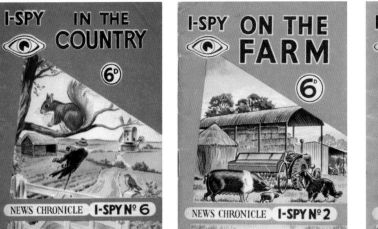

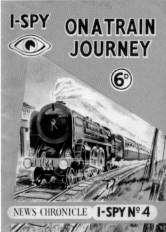

I-Spy Books

above right
I-Spy Secret Codes, vital
for covert messaging,
and the *I-Spy handbook*,
which gave helpful
suggestions for your
Redskin name. I could
never see myself as
'Silent One' or even
'Beaver Cub'

below
How to greet another
Redskin

We are perhaps used to seeing the present-day reincarnation of these little books, a brilliant and well-executed idea sponsored by Michelin. They are glossy and printed in full colour and so up-to-date we wouldn't be at all surprised to see I-Spy Retail Parks or I-Spy iPods. The idea is to look out for things, enter the location in the relevant book and score points. The originals were far less sophisticated – cheap paper editions with a coloured cover and forty-eight pages of superb line drawings of everything from roadside milk churn platforms (score: 10) to hospital sphygmo-manometers (score: 30).

The I-Spy Tribe was founded by a former headmaster who wrote an I-Spy column for the *News Chronicle* (later the *Daily Mail*) and planned the books. The whole phenomenon evolved around a faux Indian tribe of which Charles Warrell (later Arnold Cawthrow) was Big Chief I-Spy, with an assistant, Hawkeye.

They worked out of Wigwam-by-the-Water in Blackfriars, from where they posted out secret codes and real bird feathers if you sent in completed books signed by an adult. If you saw another Redskin in the street – identifiable by the green and white badge –, you were supposed to greet each other by raising up the palm of your hand and saying 'How!'. This only happened to me once. I was in Woolworths and a small boy with myopic NHS spectacles came up to me and shouted out the greeting. I'd forgotten I was wearing my badge and just stared at him in deep embarrassment.

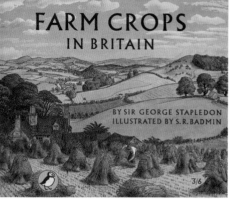

Puffin Picture Books

above
Two Puffin Picture Books
illustrated by S.R. Badmin

opposite
Detail from the cover of
S.R. Badmin's *Village and
Town*

Noel Carrington brought the idea of Puffin Picture Books to Allen Lane at Penguin Books after Country Life had turned him down in 1938. Carrington had been very impressed by the cheap, but beautifully lithographed Russian educational books for children, and by the French Père Castor books. Lane was enthusiastic and *War on the Land* appeared in 1940, the first of a series that ran to 120 titles until finishing in 1965. (*Life Histories* by Paxton Chadwick had to wait thirty years for its appearance, published in 1995 by the Penguin Collectors' Society.)

Puffin Picture Books were made twice the size of an ordinary Penguin Book, so they could be dispatched to booksellers in the space inevitably left at the top of boxes used for the standard supply of books. They normally had thirty-two pages, printed on one sheet of paper with colour lithography on one side and single colour black on the reverse. Many were printed by W.S. Cowell of Ipswich, who experimented very successfully with plastic plates that helped the illustrators (a large number of which also wrote the text) to achieve stunning effects.

One of those illustrators was S.R. Badmin, who contributed *Trees in Britain*, *Farm Crops* (with text by Sir George Stapledon) and, what is probably one of the best, *Village and Town*. I had the great privilege of meeting Mr Badmin in his West Sussex home under the Downs and he showed me the proofs of *Village and Town*. He explained that he first drew all the pictures as line drawings, then sent them off to the printer who made the plates and returned to him a number of copies printed in pale blue. On the sheets Badmin filled in the outline for each of the individual colours to be printed. He was working to meet the deadline on *Trees in Britain* as bombs fell on the railway embankment at the bottom of his garden in Sydenham.

Many Puffin Picture Book titles are superb evocations of life in post-war England; books that introduced children to architecture, natural history, engineering and even somewhat esoteric subjects, such as heraldry and coalmining. Their thin paper has made them very vulnerable to damage and excessive wear, but it's still possible to buy the more popular titles for just a few pounds.

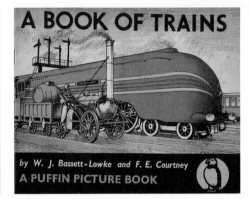

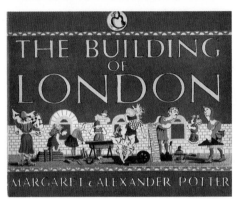

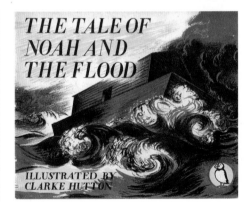

right
Lithographed illustration
from Puffin Picture Book
No. 4, *On the Farm* by
James Gardner

right
Lithographed illustration
from Puffin Picture Book
No. 71, *Pottery and its
Making* by John Thomas
and Mary Sikes

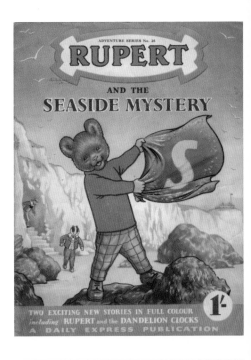

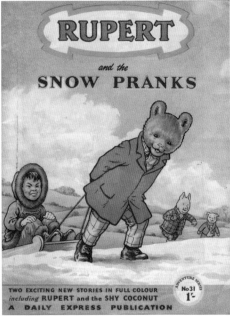

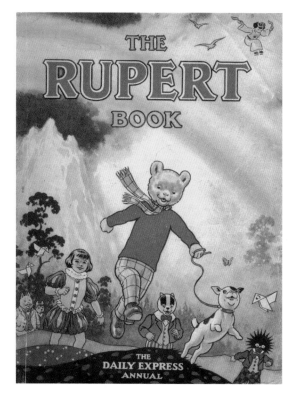

"Jump in beside me," says the man.
"And you shall travel in my van."

Rupert

This red-jumpered, golf-trousered, cricket-booted bear still appears in the *Daily Express* as he has done since Mary Tourtel's drawings first appeared in 1920. But if you want him in glorious Nutwood colour you need to buy an annual. Still faithful to the original books, Rupert and his pals have not embraced the digital age; they remain loyal to the best-loved, if

bizarre, depictions first given to them by Alfred Bestall in 1936. Mrs Bear in cotton print dress and matronly apron, Bill Badger as a 1920 Eton schoolboy and Gregory Guinea Pig as Pre-Raphaelite painter. The Pekinese Pong-Ping still wears spats and Rupert's dad plus fours. Other favourites still pop up in the picture frames – the frightening mortar-boarded schoolmaster Dr Chimp, Sergeant Growler with his flash lamp and Sailor Sam the Victorian mariner with his waxed pigtail.

The words still follow the time-honoured format of simple couplets – 'The startled pals are all still dazed / When back the pedlar runs, amazed' – under the pictures or, for those with more time and a thirst for more comprehensive information, there's the expanded version running at the foot of the page. One puzzle still remains, quite apart from the torture meted out by the origami pages, and that's Rupert's complexion. Devoid of any facial colour whatsoever in the stories, he somehow gains a hairy teddy bear look on the front covers, albeit with pink humanoid hands. Rupert the Werewolf perhaps.

opposite
If you couldn't wait for the annual, the *Daily Express* issued books in the Adventure Series with two stories in each for a shilling

above
The 1948 softback *Rupert* annual

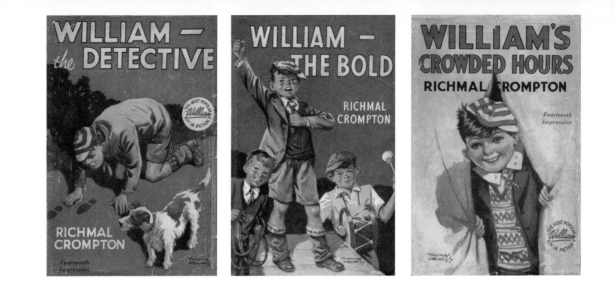

William

above and opposite
Thomas Henry's colourful
dust jackets give William
books a strong graphic
style

opposite, bottom right
A rare, if not unique sight
– William appearing to be
very happy about holding
hands with a girl. A scene
from *William and the
Evacuees*

William books were the first reading volumes
I was allowed to take out of the library. Like
many children I assumed the author, Richmal
Crompton, was a bloke, but the realisation that
he wasn't took nothing away from these
wonderful books. Incredibly they span five
decades, from the first, *Just William*, in 1922,
to the last, *William the Lawless*, published
posthumously in 1970. But William never aged,
gleefully able to be the eternal schoolboy
creating mischief around Home County villages
in thirty-eight books over fifty years. Not only
are they unique chronicles of village life –
everything from short-lease cottages inhabited
by maniacs to the arrival of wartime evacuees –
they are also genuinely funny and well written.
So good was Richmal Crompton's writing,
I learnt new, sometimes complex words just
from the context in which she used them.

The original line illustrations by Thomas
Henry have never been bettered, despite
occasional attempts to put William in Gap
clothes. William's untidiness is legendary, his
appearance – the blue and white striped cap at
an impossible angle, the red and white striped
tie badly knotted under a grubby collar that
continually wants to defy gravity – almost a
cipher for scruffiness. I've always loved the socks;
strangely cylindrical and looking as if there are
shin pads stuffed down them. The richly
colourful covers, with their red backgrounds
and yellow type, make these books immensely
collectable, but you and your Outlaws will have
to have many dubious fundraising efforts in the
Old Barn if you want to buy them in anything
like presentable condition.

JUST WILLIAM'S LUCK

RICHMAL CROMPTON

WILLIAM and THE MASKED RANGER

THE MASKED RANGER

Now Showing

RICHMAL CROMPTON

ALL THIS WEEK

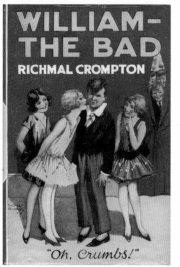

WILLIAM— THE BAD

RICHMAL CROMPTON

"Oh, Crumbs!"

WILLIAM'S TELEVISION SHOW

RICHMAL CROMPTON

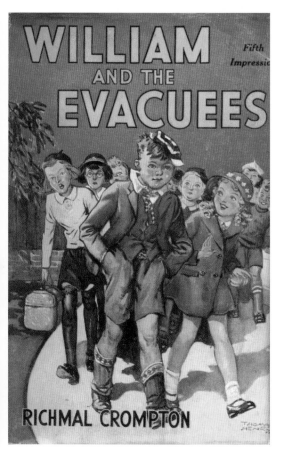

WILLIAM AND THE EVACUEES

Fifth Impression

RICHMAL CROMPTON

The Twins made a see-saw with a spoon and a potted meat jar, and had a jolly game with it.

STIGGINSONS POTTED CHICKEN & HAM

above
Seesawing mice from the tale of *Mrs Nibble*, in Lawson Wood's *The Mrs Book*

opposite
An incident in Buckingham Palace Road, illustrated by Norman Keeve in *The Modern World Book of Motors* (below)

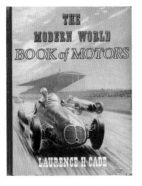

Picture This

Picture books were often the first introduction to other worlds that existed beyond the cosy confines of the nursery. The Golden Shred jar in Lawson Wood's picture was such a familiar breakfast table object I'm sure it lent credence to the notion that it was perfectly possible for two mice to seesaw on a spoon. The real puzzle is, was there really a Stigginsons brand of potted meat? And have we ever really fully understood the concept of potted meat anyway?

The Modern World Book of Motors was my rainy day standby book. In its pages I marvelled at firemen with Merryweather engines attempting to put out a church fire; I was thrilled at Nuvolari struggling with his Auto Union racing car. But the picture opposite was equally guaranteed to get my heart pounding. There was no story, just a caption: 'A daring feat performed by a police inspector in Buckingham Palace Road, when he jumped from his car at high speed and prevented bandits from

escaping.' I was so entranced with this image I cajoled elder brothers, pals, passing strangers, anybody to help me re-enact the scene using four dining room chairs set out to emulate the cars. We would take it in turns to be either the copper (in my dad's trilby) or the truncheon-wielding bandit (in one of my dad's raincoats), leaping from chair to chair whilst the 'drivers' made screeching swerving noises and wildly exaggerated steering wheel manoeuvres.

HOW TO WATCH CRICKET

There were no score cards to be had,
Cushions for folk to hire;
Only we saw the butcher's lad
Bowl out the Village Squire
'The Village Pitch', G.D. Martineau

above right
The Wisden Almanack
Cricketers, designed in
1938 by Eric Ravilious
and still in use

opposite
Detail from an illustration
on the spine of *The
Skipper of the XI* by John
Barnett

There's a cliché which, no matter how much it
is overused, commentators on the English
scene will not stop trotting out again and again.
And that's 'cricket and warm beer'. Nobody
ever queries the 'warm beer' part. I know that if
a landlord or barmaid ever pulled me a pint of
'warm beer' it would be sent straight back, but
I suppose beer is warm compared with tasteless
and frozen fizzy lagers. Beer, as any dedicated
drinker knows, should be served cooled. This is
a minor digression, however important, but try
giving a cricketer who's been at the crease for
three hours on a hot Saturday a 'warm beer'.

Cricket is of course as English as a tin of
Colman's Mustard. John Arlott, once the Voice
of Cricket, reckoned in his *The Picture of Cricket*
that the game has been played in England for at
least three hundred years, and makes the very
valid point that not only were stumps drawn at
the end of play on the cricket pitches of public
schools but equally could be found drawn in
chalk on countless slum walls. He also admits,
thankfully for me, that the game 'is perhaps, of
them all the least susceptible of precise analysis.'
It is widely recognised that the Hambledon
players in mid-eighteenth-century Hampshire
were the first great cricket club; a team made up

of farmers, innkeepers, cobblers, builders and a
potter, brought together by the local squire. And
although this was a 'professional' team, paid for
by the club members culled from the
surrounding gentry, it formed the basis for the
village cricket that is my main focus for this
chapter. (I must beg forgiveness for the
parochial nature of my images but, like everyone
else, I plead the extenuating circumstances of
the 'summer' weather of 2007.) Local cricket
somehow still manages to maintain the values
that are all too often lost in today's professional
game. Television companies fall over each other
to deprive 'terrestrial' viewers of the opportunity
to watch test matches, except in meaningless
late night edits, and sponsorship ruins cricket
shirts and cricket grounds alike. I don't think
you get much money changing hands behind
the pavilion (not for cricket anyway), although I
did hear alarming reports in one village that
some committees are not above bringing in
hired hands from outside, like gunslingers. But
at least village cricket upholds the wearing of
cricket 'whites'; one is never confronted by
players dressed in multi-coloured shell suits
covered in abysmal graphics, unless the wicket
keeper has forgotten to change.

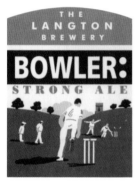

above
Bowler Strong Ale pump
clip from the Langton
Brewery in Leicestershire

right and opposite, left
Ladybird Book *The Story
of Cricket* with cover and
title page illustrations by
Jack Matthew

opposite, right
John Arlott's King Penguin
book *The Picture of
Cricket*, with cover by
Lynton Lamb, 1955

opposite, top
Puffin Picture Book
No. 109, *How to Play
Cricket*, with cover by
Leonard Hagerty, 1957

Settling into the Crease

I must first state my own fielding position
clearly. I love the *idea* of cricket, avidly watch
test matches when I can, and village fixtures,
but lack a knowledge about the finer points of
the game that is breathtaking in its coverage.
When I try to join in conversations about the
game, I am frequently humoured by my cricket
playing friends; I lurk about on the boundary
of village matches, often getting distracted by
the tea urn in the pavilion or falling into
conversation with a girl sitting on the roller. It
must stem from schooldays – never getting
picked for a team until I was the last
despondent boy staring at his dirty plimsolls,
then being shouted at when I clumsily missed
catch after catch or knocked the bails off with
the first stroke of my bat. But I was nevertheless
encouraged by my elder brother Andrew, who
took me to see Frank Tyson bowl at Grace Road
in Leicester, and who put an Abram Games'
Festival of Britain sticker on the family bat used
in garden test matches. His bedtime reading
was the *Playfair Annual*, always had Howzat
cricket game hexagonal dice in his blazer
pocket and insisted we play on our back lawn
with a proper leather ball that hurt like hell
when it regularly hit me instead of the bat. It
also had a far more devastating and

mesmerising effect when it sailed through the
unopened kitchen window.

So although not very good at it, and never
being able to distinguish 'mid-offs' from 'short
extra cover points', cricket is my game of
choice. My passions do, however, tend to pitch
alarmingly away from 'short square leg' towards
the salmon and cucumber sandwiches and
pavilion building styles.

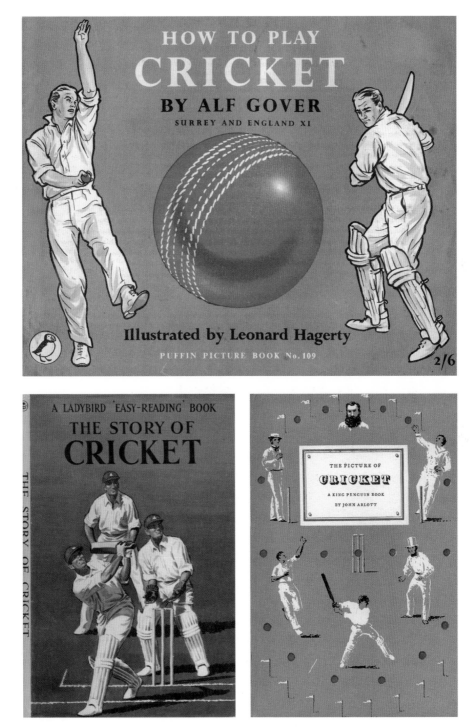

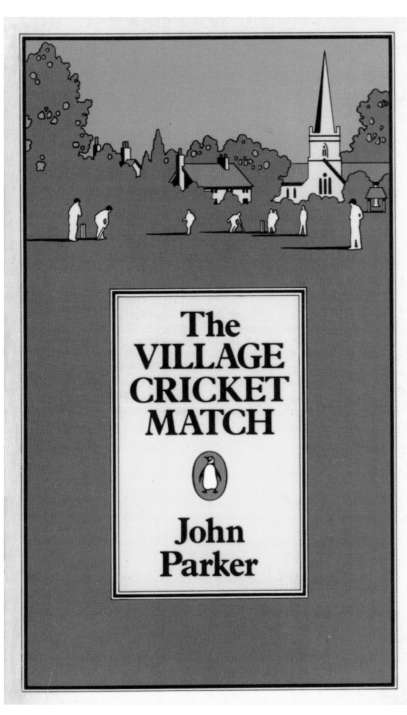

John Gorham (1937–2001) was probably the biggest single influence on me as a graphic designer. His work for Penguin books (and indeed for films and stamps) is legendary. Everything he did was handcrafted – no mouse mats for John – and imbued with an innate sense of Englishness. None more so perhaps than these covers for books depicting the game he loved. John once played for Uxbridge

above
Detail from the illustration for *The Penguin Cricketer's Companion*, 1981

left
Cover design and illustration for *The Village Cricket Match*, 1978

above
A scene from Harry
Huntingdon's *A Hard-
Fought Game:* 'The
leather sped between the
bowler and mid-off and
reached the boundary'

right
Fielding at East Langton,
Leicestershire

Out on the Boundary

In John Parker's *The Village Cricket Match*, a
character called Trine is positioned on the
outfield, the sort of distance from the main
action that was also my own preference. Just as
I was continually distracted by double-headed
express steam trains rushing from Leicester to St
Pancras at the end of the school playing field, so
too Trine's attention is drawn to two pretty girls
laying out a rug in the grass on the other side of
the boundary fence. As he adjusts his position to
get a better look, there's a shout of, 'Catch it
Trine,' from the epicentre of the game, and for a
split second my hero thinks, 'Catch what?'.

Reading this episode again reminded me of
company cricket matches that took place in
North London in the 1980s. When fielding, our
charismatic but authoritarian chairman always
stood resolutely out on the boundary (deep mid-
on, I think it's called), usually with a Rothmans
on the go. He always made sure that he was not
too far away from another similarly placed
fielder, and if the ball should dare to come within
his remit he would take the cigarette out of his
mouth in order to languidly say, 'Get that would
you?'. There was also a rumour that one of the
account directors, who in a previous existence
had everyone running about after him in one of

Hereford's best known cider companies, had
asked if he could have a boy from the post room
to run for him if, perchance, he made contact
with the ball whilst batting.

VISITORS

left
East Langton Cricket
Club Pavilion,
Leicestershire

**opposite, clockwise
from top left**
Uppingham School,
Rutland; Bournville,
Birmingham; Stanway,
Gloucestershire;
Cadnam, Hampshire;
Blankney, Lincolnshire

Peripheral Visions

above and opposite, top left
Cricket roller and sight screen at Gumley in Leicestershire. Only very recently was I told by a cricketing friend that they're called 'sight screens' and not 'side screens', which I've called them all my life, as if they fixed to a motorcycle sidecar

above right
Essential traffic management on the road crossing the Gumley ground

opposite, top right
Sorting out the score board at Wing, Rutland c. 1990

opposite, bottom
Motorised sophistication, the roller at Tillingham in Essex

Round the outside of the cricket pitch are many delights to distract the idle spectator from his deliberations about 'off breaks' and 'legs before wickets'. The big white sight screens are there to give the bowler a clear, uninterrupted view of the wicket and the batsmen about to receive his ball, rather than of the spectacle of men who should know better chatting up girls on cricket rollers. Always on iron wheels, like a mobile shepherd's hut, they are often weighted down against inclement English weather by sandbags.

The wicket is of course the sacred territory of groundsmen, who, I'm sure, must grind their teeth like gang mowers when players dare to set foot on it. It is stared at and prodded like a prize bull at a cattle market, a 22-yard stretch of turf that more resembles a pale beige hallway carpet than grass. The heavyweight presence at pre-match wicket rituals is the cricket roller, usually to be found gently rusting in the long grass at the playing field edge. The team spirit that pulls together in the final critical overs is tested to the full in the pulling of this behemoth over the wicket. So jealously guarded are the individual

characteristic of rollers, Uppingham School took theirs to Borth in Wales when typhoid struck the school in 1876. The railway had not yet reached the town, so the roller was trundled down to Seaton Junction station for loading, a distance of some 5 miles, and then was trundled, somewhat more slowly, back up to this hilltop Rutland town.

But the one item of cricket furniture that players always ensure is within their vision is the scoreboard. Being somewhat interested in lettering, these mobile figures have always fascinated me – everything from individual letters hung out on pegs after sorting (as seen here in Wing) to clattering pieces of painted iron flipping over to either shouts of glee or sighs of disappointment. Always with a tweed-jacketed figure in the gloom behind, bent over the religiously kept scorebook. A dark inner sanctum ripe for a murder of the Midsomer variety or, even more macabre, the perversity of apparent spontaneous combustion as witnessed in the opening scenes of Alan Bates's film *The Shout* (1978).

Gentlemen and Players

above and opposite, top
East Langton at home,
playing Croft. To find a
perfect match of batsman
and bowler I took
numerous photographs at
both ends of the wicket.
Of course the two best
shots were both at the
same end. So I thought
I'd cheat and reverse the
bowler, forgetting that
this heinous act suddenly
rendered him left-handed

Most players are gentlemen now of course. But some of the most emotionally loaded matches must have been those played between The Hall and The Rest. Here was the common ground, in many cases the only ground, except in trench warfare, where the otherwise very clear distinctions between the classes were blurred.

Who can forget those memorable scenes in Joseph Losey's *The Go-Between* (1970) where the village take on their masters at Brandham Hall? Mr Maudsley (Michael Gough) from the Hall, paired with his son, trying to steal runs and being continually stopped from doing so, 'thwarted by Denys's raised arm, which shot up like policeman's.' Tenant farmer Ted Burgess (Alan Bates on top form) knocking the ball all over the ground, watched by the baleful stare of Mrs Maudsley (a truly frightening performance from Margaret Leighton), who has her

suspicions that he's also knocking off her daughter Marian (aah, Julie Christie). And, of course, Leo Colston (Dominic Guard), saving the day for the Hall by catching Burgess out with a heart-stopping catch and then singing for his supper in the flag bedecked village hall. But one instinctively feels that this is a real match going on, of which we see only edited highlights. The screenplay from L.P. Hartley's book was written by cricket buff Harold Pinter, who almost certainly couldn't have resisted picking up a bat or ball himself. Losey was insistent that everybody immersed themselves in the period (1900), even down to their staying in dressing-up clothes for the duration of filming.

Village cricket grounds are still one of the most 'level playing fields' we could hope for in our society. Where blacksmiths once faced viscounts, photographers now bowl out

right
More action at East Langton. Fred Trueman reckoned this to be amongst the very best of village cricket pitches

below
Another decisive moment from Harry Huntingdon's *A Hard-Fought Game*

barristers (in my dreams), and the conversation in the pavilion or village pub still goes on long after the stumps are drawn in evening light. For me, locked in the impotence of my loitering with intent by the boundary, it's the almost eternal *look* of village cricket that never goes away. Brian Jones in his poem 'Cricket for Christmas' has it about right:

These players, like white legends of themselves,
Step soundless on to May green. Leaves
come big as hands from buds. The numbers
flower from winter scoreboard zeros.
Cricket is always the memory of cricket.

A POST BOX COLLECTION

*...Like the postmen who deliver our letters, the boxes in which we mail them
are regarded with the same personal feelings we normally reserve for our
oldest and most valued household possessions.*

From the Preface to *The Letter Box* (Jean Young Farrugia), Anthony Wedgwood Benn

opposite
Front cover of a pre-war
postcard album

With their imposing, but simple shape and emphatic colour scheme, post boxes are as unmistakable as original red telephone kiosks and yellow fire hydrants. Possibly they are the first item of street furniture that a child recognises; I remember being held up by my mother in order to send a letter skimming into the darkness of the pillar box at the end of our road, perhaps not understanding that it could reappear as if by magic virtually anywhere in the world.

Standing on pavements like guardsmen, set into brick walls or strapped to tarred telegraph poles, they are one of the most potent symbols of communication. Post boxes mean letters, simple as that. (We struggle to find anything as succinct for emails.) And the ubiquitous presence of these iron castings is all Anthony Trollope's fault. Long before he dashed off *The Barchester Chronicles* he was instrumental in introducing the idea to the Channel Islands in 1852; it did not reach the mainland until the following year, in Botchergate, Carlisle. The first pillar box of our present queen's reign appeared in Whitehall near the Horseguards' Parade in November 1952.

Right from the start they were emblazoned with Royal coats of arms and ciphers, so we can always apply a rough chronology to them. (Even

Edward VIII had his cipher cast into a handful of boxes before he decided he didn't want the job.) The designs have been as varied as the districts they serve; everything from the 1866 hexagonal Penfold box topped out with acanthus leaves, to the fat double boxes first cast by Handysides of Derby in 1898. Pillar boxes near post offices appeared with beautifully lettered cream oval signs with pointing arrows; remote rural lanes were punctuated with round-topped, curved-top and humped-back boxes on grass verges.

I believe there's an agreement between the Royal Mail and English Heritage to preserve post boxes in the form we know and love; a timely measure in these manic days when we fully expect to wake up and find everything's been painted beige and is owned by the Dutch. I think this possibly irrational fear made me start yet another collection, not just photographs of post boxes that appealed to me, but equally their frequent use in printed ephemera, some of which you'll find on the following pages. And did you ever wonder how pillar boxes stay upright? Like the proverbial iceberg there's apparently almost as much of them below ground as on top.

Post-Cards

I Wonder !

I wonder if you
ever meet
A thing like this
upon the street.
If so, please will
you tell me why
You always seem
to pass it by ?

Allan Junior.

No. 290.

left
An illustration by Lawson
Wood from *Princess
Marie Jose's Children's
Book*, sold during the
First World War in aid
of Belgian babies born
behind Allied lines

above and opposite
Postcards from the post.
Suffragette Militant
Millicent and her
kerosine (*sic*) – sent from
Nottingham to Spilsby,
Lincolnshire in 1914 – now
cuts a more treacherous
than comic figure

JUST A LITTLE CARD ——
    REALLY NOTHING IN IT
SCRIBBLE THE ADDRESS ——
    DOESN'T TAKE A MINUTE
JUST A LITTLE STAMP ——
    BUT A HA'PENNY TO PAY
BUT IT SHOWS YOU'RE NOT FORGOTTEN
    WHEN YOU ARE FAR AWAY.

*Life is short—as time will show
If you don't get this—please
let me know!*

FULLY PROTECTED.

THEY CALL ME "MILITANT MILLICENT
WITH HER LITTLE KEROSINE CAN"!

YOU CAN SAFELY TRUST THIS
FELLOW TO BRING ME A MESSAGE

I'M SORRY
I MISSED THE POST!

*I WAS GOING TO SEND A LETTER
  BUT I THINK A POST-CARD'S BETTER,
SO I'M SENDING YOU THIS FRIENDLY LITTLE LINE;
  IT'S NOT SO VERY PRETTY
  AND IT'S NOT SO VERY WITTY
BUT IT SHOWS I DON'T FORGET YOU ALL THE TIME!*

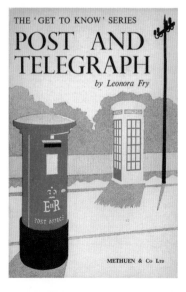

left
Pillar-box red on a children's road safety booklet, 1950

bottom right
Onoto ink bookmark

bottom centre
Front cover for another children's book, 1954

bottom left
The slightly fey world of Tony Meeuwissen, one of an award winning set of stamps for Christmas, 1983

opposite, top and bottom left
Party invitations

opposite, top right
An irresistible image for the *Post Office Magazine*

opposite, bottom right
Christmas postcard

THANK YOU FOR YOUR KIND
INVITATION TO THE PARTY
ON_____ AT_____
WILL BE DELIGHTED TO COME.

I'm posting this myself, dear,
I'm so eager to secure you,
My Party would be no success
Without you I assure you.

POST OFFICE
MAGAZINE

NOVEMBER, 1952

FIRST POST

PRICE THREEPENCE

HOPING THIS WILL REACH YOU.
WITH BEST CHRISTMAS GREETINGS

Letters sometimes go astray:
Please be careful what you say!

NEVER MENTION SHIPS

Issued by the British Ship Adoption Society

above
Hitler waits behind a jumbo-sized pillar box, waiting to pick up the shipping news. One of a series of wartime posters by Fougasse, characterised by his trademark red border and hand-drawn lettering

right
Cover of Geographia's London Postal Map. I wonder if the Royal Mail ever had a vehicle sporting the number plate GPO 123. I like to think so

"GEOGRAPHIA"
POSTAL MAP
OF
LONDON

3/6

INCLUDING THE POSTAL REGION OUTSIDE THE LONDON DISTRICT

"GEOGRAPHIA" LTD.
167, Fleet Street, LONDON, E.C.4

above
Self-promotion illustration by Andrew Davidson

left
A childhood favourite for many children. The pillar box has a cut-out window to show the Toy Post stamps inside

below
The cigarettes I would have smoked if I had been around in the 1920s

opposite, clockwise
from top left
Posh Box, Greenwich,
S.E. London; How they
post letters in West
Lulworth, Dorset;
Yaldham, Kent; Hastings,
East Sussex; Stansted,
Kent

above left
Trinity Street, Cambridge

above right
King John Farm
near Sutton Bridge,
Lincolnshire

far right
Woburn, Bedfordshire

right
Sibthorpe,
Nottinghamshire

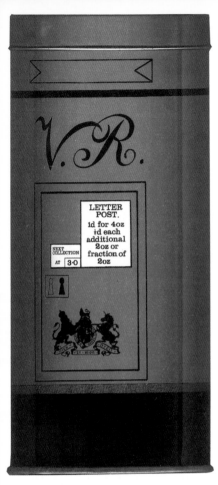

opposite
A collection of tin money boxes. Worthy of note is the pottery pillar box by Benjamin Ashley (6), made for his father, including his own BA cipher scored into the clay

above
Illustration by Charles Folkard for *Mother Goose's Nursery Rhymes*

right
An early twentieth-century Onoto ink bottle. The clever thing is that the black base of the pillar box only revealed itself when the clear glass bottle was filled with ink

below
Back cover of the *Look!* booklet

ENGLISHMEN'S CASTLES

After my work in the City, I like to be at home! What's the good of a home,
if you are never in it? 'Home Sweet Home'; that's my motto.
Diary of a Nobody, George and Weedon Grossmith

opposite
Detail from an Oxo
advertisement of 1951.
The headline reads, 'It's
an odd house where
there's no Oxo'

Have you ever thought about how many different houses you've lived in? Of course the older you are (like me) the total will be a lot more than if you're sixteen and still living with mum and dad. But I don't really think of them as houses as much as homes, in my case not so much struggling up the property ladder as wilfully sliding down the property snake. As a result, I've had the immense privilege of making my home in everything from one half of a pink Elizabethan farmhouse in remote Essex to a tiny red brick Arts and Crafts flat in Chiswick; a limestone gamekeeper's lodge backed up against woods in Northamptonshire to a gothicky diapered brickwork farmworker's cottage in deepest Leicestershire. In fact the only downside has obviously been in improving the wealth of my landlords and their agents, but the one time I actually bought anything I looked out with dismay at thirty others exactly the same and all my furniture warped because of a newfangled thing called central heating.

We are always fascinated by other people's homes, and not just in the style sections of colour supplements. Who has been able to resist a quick sidelong glance through a downstairs window at night on passing a house where the curtains are not drawn against the night? (At least I hope it isn't just me.) But it's the outside we see most, and if you have more than just a passing interest in buildings then the ordinary English home is represented in a bewildering catalogue of house styles to enjoy and appreciate. Not just chocolate-box thatched cottages, but also the suburban semi-detached or indeed the suburban not-attached-to-anything. I love estate houses, not just the ruthless rebuilding by megalomaniacs who wanted the old village removed from the sight lines of the great house, but also the altruistic endeavours of industrialists.

This chapter isn't a history of domestic architecture, just a record of some of the houses and cottages that I've been sent out to photograph or that have simply appealed to me on my journeys. But all of them are somebody's home. So don't stare too much over the hedge and don't press your noses up against sitting room windows – particularly at night –, unless of course you want to see the living accommodation at your local nick.

Comings and Goings

above left
Blatherwycke,
Northamptonshire

above centre
Attingham Park,
Shropshire

above right
Eccleston Hill Lodge,
Eaton Hall, Cheshire

There is something fascinating about gate lodges. Out on the fringes of private estates they give clues as to what is to come or, to quote the title of Tim Mowl's and Brian Earnshaw's seminal work on the subject, a *Trumpet at a Distant Gate*. Around ever since the castle demanded a defensive outpost or an abbey a buffer zone to keep out undesirables, lodges had their golden age during the eighteenth century, when landscaping and architectural experiment included building entrances that reflected the tastes of the owner of the Big House. The classic lodge matured into what has become our popular image of them; homes for aged retainers fumbling with keys on windswept nights to open wrought-iron gates for impatient masters. I must admit to getting a bit obsessive about these little houses a few years back, skulking about suspiciously in the lanes outside country estates like Jude the Obscure. In fact I was waiting for rays of sunlight to hit the right place in order to photograph them for a little book on the subject, but many of the keepers and householders were very understanding, once I'd told them I wasn't an axe murderer.

Blatherwycke is exactly as Juliet Smith described it in her *Shell Guide to Northamptonshire*, imagining the coaches of the Staffords and O'Brians rumbling homeward down a drive that 'would provide an ideal setting for the opening of an M.R. James ghost story.' Ghosts indeed, for Blatherwycke Hall has now gone, demolished after the deprivations caused by wartime requisitioning, leaving only an 1876 lodge announcing a haunting park with a Norman church lost in the trees.

Back Lodge in Attingham Park, near Shrewsbury is a little 'gothick' gem, which, as its name implies, is not on the main driveway but demurely tucked up against chestnut trees on an outer edge. Eaton Hall, on the other hand, trumpets at every given opportunity on the intensely private Grosvenor Estate of the Duke of Westminster to the south of Chester. I was taken around under close but friendly guard, but wanted to break loose and run about all over

above left
Midelney Place, Curry
Rivel, Somerset

above centre
Lilford Hall,
Northamptonshire

above right
Norney Grange,
Shackleford, Surrey

below right
Detail of the Eccleston
Hill Lodge, Eaton Hall

John Douglas's 1882 Eccleston Hill Lodge. This has everything – brick and tile hung turrets, Cheshire magpie half-timbering and duotone sandstone studded with Grosvenor heraldry; perfect reference material for illustrating a William Morris fantasy. I get something of the same feeling – but in a more convivial mood – at the perfectly proportioned gatehouse to Midelney Place at Curry Rivel in Somerset.

South of Oundle in Northamptonshire is a pair of late eighteenth-century 'mirror image' lodges in Jacobean style, which announce Lilford Hall. Both are angled to the road and hall driveway, the better for gaining an uninterrupted view of all the comings and goings. Living here must be like adopting the lifestyle of Beatrix Potter's country mouse. And, keeping with literary allusion, the oriel window of Voysey's fabulous 1897 lodge for Norney Grange near Shackleford in Surrey always puts in my mind Walter de la Mare's 'The Listeners':

'Is there anybody there?' he said.
But no one descended to the Traveller;
No head from the leaf-fringed sill
Leaned over and looked into his grey eyes…
But only a host of phantom listeners…

Model Behaviour

above left
Tony Meeuwissen's exquisite cover for Gillian Darley's *Villages of Vision*, 1978

above right
Estate cottages in Buckminster, Leicestershire

This isn't about those model villages like the wonderfully English Bekonscot – where the local newspaper reported the flames from a house fire as being seen from 3 feet away –, but life-size estates. Elsewhere in this book I've talked about houses that were introduced into the urban environment as the result of philanthropic or aesthetic ideals – at Bournville, Port Sunlight and Bedford Park. Out in the countryside the same thinking – sometimes altruistic, often as a result of megalomania – has produced estate villages and dwellings of architectural merit that stand out as models of community. At its simplest the ideal will be seen in villages where all the front doors, and indeed all painted surfaces, are the same colour. Everything from economy bucket-white on the Biggin and Benefield Estate in Northamptonshire to the sumptuously-rich burgundy seen in Buckminster in north-east Leicestershire.

Essentially the estate village is one that has been planned, as opposed to having grown organically from early settlements. Almost always the result of land ownership by one man, the village's early narrative is described by Gillian Darley in her brilliant *Villages of Vision*: 'An ancient collection of disintegrating hovels would be removed from the parkland and replaced by a pristine new line of cottages.' Often criticised now by revisionist historians as nothing more than oppressive paternalism, the villages nevertheless have a cohesive quality and visual appeal from which today's greedy developers, who cram pastiches of all eras into overpriced housing estates, could learn much.

This sense of community is particularly strong where buildings are designed as a homogenous whole. On the B1188 between Ruskington and Lincoln the attention is suddenly focused on the houses on each side of the road in Blankney. Laid out in the 1830s and '40s by W.A. Nicholson, these are groups of Tudor-style dwellings, stone built with spruce green paintwork and low privet hedges framed by white post-and-rail fences. But the house that presided over it all, featured in Sir Osbert Sitwell's *The Scarlet Tree*, was burnt down following the RAF's wartime occupation.

The once great estate surrounding the villages of Upper and Lower Benefield now

above left
One of John Nash's 1811 cottages for Quaker banker John Harford in Blaise Hamlet, near Bristol

above right
The old post office, Blankney, Lincolnshire

below
Gamekeeping turned poaching. Chesterfield Lodge, near Oundle

resounds with the noise of the cash register, as the housing stock is sold off and long-term tenants are evicted in order to 'maximise earning potential'. But there are still reminders of a more gracious era out in the fields – farms, granges and lodges in locally quarried silver limestone. Backed up against Oundle Wood is a Georgian gamekeeper's cottage, built in 1820 as a hunting lodge. One of England's best known keepers, the late Harry Churchill, lived here for over forty years, his rearing pens and paraphernalia spread about like hens around a coop. After two early Christmases at the lodge Harry planted for his daughter the festive trees that grew into wonderfully tall specimens out in the garden and meadow. One has been recently and ruthlessly axed; just admiring trees doesn't earn any money you see. Thank goodness there are enlightened individuals who care a little more. Take a look at Blaise Hamlet at Henbury near Bristol if you have any doubts.

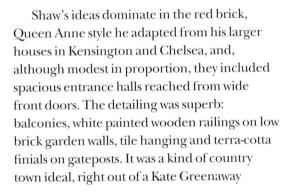

Red Brick Aesthetics

above left
Detail from a Kate
Greenaway illustration
in *Little Ann*, 1883

above centre
Chestnuts and tile
hanging in Marlborough
Crescent

above right
Comforting domestic
detail in red brick and
white paint

below right
Terra-cotta and brick
fence post

Many years ago I was driving out of London down the Bath Road, intent on getting on the M4 for Dorset or somewhere. My girlfriend suddenly said: 'Quick, turn down here, there's something I must show you.' Always willing to oblige immediately to such a request I turned off into what became one of my most frequented haunts in London and indeed, for a few years, my home.

In the mid 1870s speculator Jonathan Carr spotted a 24-acre estate, known as Bedford Park, for sale as his train pulled out of Turnham Green station. He asked architects E.W. Godwin and Coe & Robinson to produce plans for small detached and semi-detached villas on the land but, after the drawings were given a pasting by the highly influential *Building News,* he got Norman Shaw involved and the earliest true garden suburb emerged amongst the trees, many of which were preserved because the street pattern was arranged around them. Shaw was employed first as architect and then as consultant, and his influence can be seen everywhere.

Shaw's ideas dominate in the red brick, Queen Anne style he adapted from his larger houses in Kensington and Chelsea, and, although modest in proportion, they included spacious entrance halls reached from wide front doors. The detailing was superb: balconies, white painted wooden railings on low brick garden walls, tile hanging and terra-cotta finials on gateposts. It was a kind of country town ideal, right out of a Kate Greenaway

above and right
The variety of house design and detailing in Bedford Park, Chiswick, West London

illustration, and indeed the area was fallen upon by artists and writers, anxious to find an affordable William Morris utopia amidst the chestnuts and laurels. The *St James Gazette* of 17 December 1881 had a go at them with, 'Biled lobster 'ouses… where men may lead a chaste correct aesthetical existence,' and G.K. Chesterton – who met his future wife at Bedford Park's debating club – couldn't resist setting a novel here, *The Man Who Was Thursday.*

As night follows day somewhere as good as this inevitably caught the piggy eyes of the new breed of developers and, in 1963, John Betjeman was instrumental in the formation of the Bedford Park Society, which saved the estate for posterity. I thought an extraordinary meeting of the committee would be convened one night when my supper guest Mr Hooper rode off into the night on his bicycle to Hammersmith without first detaching the security chain from the garden fence.

Health and Efficiency

George Orwell got hot under his collar about the garden city. In his 1937 *Road to Wigan Pier* he wrote that Letchworth in Hertfordshire had attracted, '… every fruit juice drinker, nudist, sandal wearer, sex maniac, Quaker, nature cure quack, pacifist and feminist in England.' In addition to possessing these startling predilections, the Letchworth community worked in a big corset factory and talked about it in the evening in a pub that only served Cadbury's Drinking Chocolate and Cydrax. Not my idea of Utopia exactly, but as the first doors were opened in 1903, this first garden city attracted those wearing shorts and artistic smocks to the Arts and Crafts houses and green open spaces. As my friend Philip Wilkinson says, 'to get on with their yoghurt knitting.'

The concept of garden cities was to bring about self-supporting communities, who would live in houses close by to the industries and businesses that had also been imported as part of the infrastructure, all in a rural setting.

Raymond Unwin and Barry Parker's Letchworth was followed by Welwyn Garden City in 1919, which was later graced with Louis de Soisson's superb 1935 Shredded Wheat Factory. In contrast to the garden city, the garden suburb did not rely on having new local factories, but still enjoyed a vital sense of community. Hampstead Garden Suburb, which is, along with Bedford Park, perhaps the most visually satisfying of them all, was first conceived by Dame Henrietta Barnett in 1907.

It grew in a series of estates, which evolved around the principle that the individual was much improved by property investment, but at £5 for the down payment the ownership of a house was still firmly in the preserve of the office clerk and skilled worker. The great and good in architecture got involved right from the start: Lutyens, Baillie Scott and old hands Parker and Unwin. Englishmen's castles indeed. Mother switching on the lamp in the bay window, listening for the click of the garden gate as father walks in from the Underground station. Take a look at a garden suburb today; you don't need to wear sandals with socks or take your clothes off to be at home there anymore. Not unless you want to.

top left
House in Norton Road, Letchworth, Hertfordshire

top right
Mortgage Corporation symbol

above
Double garden gates, Hampstead Garden Suburb

above left
Welwyn Garden City,
Hertfordshire

above right
Hampstead Garden
Suburb, North London

Chatteris, Cambridgeshire

Chicheley Hall, Buckinghamshire

Rievaulx, North Yorkshire

Lowesby, Leicestershire

Mapledurham, Oxfordshire

Charterville, Minster Lovell, Oxfordshire

Wibtoft, Warwickshire

Bignor, West Sussex

Briston, Norfolk

Whitstable, Kent

Uppark, West Sussex

Swaffham Prior, Cambridgeshire

Makeshift Permanence

above
Nissen-Petren houses at
West Camel near Yeovil,
Somerset

opposite, top
Corrugated iron in east
Dorset

opposite, bottom
Uni-Seco prefabs in
Catford, South London

I suppose the first prefabricated structure was a tent somewhere, but the prefabs that interest me are those buildings constructed in a factory, brought by truck to the location and quickly erected on site. The First World War saw an unprecedented demand for housing troops, and the countryside witnessed semi-circle hoops of corrugated iron being anchored down in army camps, the very first Nissen huts. They could fit in the back of a 3-ton truck and the record time for six men to erect one was 1 hour 27 minutes. Normally they took 4 hours. The Second World War saw them arriving on airfields, but not before the idea was adapted in Nissen-Petren houses, a 1925 row of which line up below the A303 at West Camel in Somerset.

Corrugated-iron houses are probably most likely to be seen painted bright red, in places like New Zealand or the Falkland Islands; pioneering domesticity where home arrived on a cargo ship. But occasionally we will see the idea of prefabricated metal houses expressing itself in some truly idiosyncratic buildings in the English countryside. I particularly like the green painted cottage I came across in the Purbeck Hills in Dorset, comfortably set amidst the pines and neatly trimmed hedges. Corrugated iron never became the material of choice for makeshift housing, possibly because of the cowshed perceptions of the public. But for the wartime homeless our most popular image of rapidly built homes, the classic prefab, was welcomed with utility-clothed arms.

Introduced to meet the heavy demand for housing in post-war England, the prefab was immediately taken to heart, ready-made bungalows with bathrooms and kitchens already installed. They were only ever meant to be temporary, but many became much-loved survivors. That is until our old friend Dev the Developer and his mates on the council realised that two pricey houses could be built on the plot

of one prefab, and they slowly started to disappear. One of the last groups of prefabs in existence, built in 1946–47 by prisoners of war, can still be seen on the Excalibur Estate in Catford in South London. But hurry, the Save Our Prefabs stickers are going up in the windows and Union flags are flying as Lewisham council revs up the bulldozer.

OPEN HOUSE *by Louis Golding*

HOMES
AND
GARDENS

MARCH 1945
Price 1/6

left
Planning for a brighter future, the March 1945 issue of *Homes and Gardens*

opposite, clockwise from top left
Cerebos Salt advertisement from 1953; Wallcharm paint schemes booklet *c.* 1950 (I wonder if the food in the oven was given a quick coat of Surf Green too); Mother and son plan their new Bayko home, 1958; and a sticker originally attached to a letterhead spelling out Pilchers' quotation for linseed oil putty, March 1929

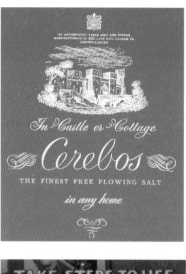

By Appointment Table Salt and Pepper Manufacturers to the late King George VI Cerebos Limited

In Castle or Cottage
Cerebos
THE FINEST FREE FLOWING SALT

in any home

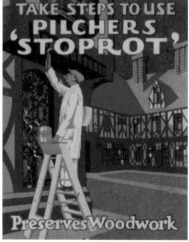

TAKE STEPS TO USE
**PILCHERS
'STOPROT'**

Preserves Woodwork

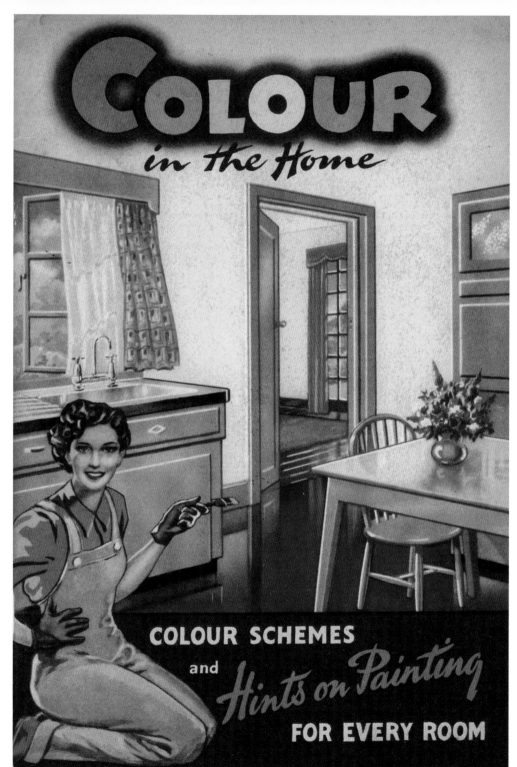

Colour
in the Home

COLOUR SCHEMES
and
Hints on Painting
FOR EVERY ROOM

Great Adaptations

'Recycling' is such a right-on buzzword these days we tend to forget that it's been going on with buildings ever since windmill sails stopped turning or railway stations saw the last passenger train disappearing down the track. There must be great kudos in saying, 'Of course this used to be a lighthouse,' and your guest saying, 'Oh, I wondered why all your furniture was curved.' It probably started with needs-must fixations after the First World War – old Southern Railway carriages taken off their wheels and dragged across the hot shingle at Dungeness, plotland shacks metamorphosing into bungalows amongst the trees in steep North Down valleys. But one only has to think of Peggotty's boat grounded on a Yarmouth beach in Dickens's *David Copperfield* to realise that recycling has always gone on.

Water towers have always found favour with the Unusual Homemaker. Something to do with them having massively strong supporting walls and, of course, wonderful views over your neighbours' gardens. The House in the Clouds

at Thorpeness is the highlight of the Suffolk holiday village that Stuart Ogilvy started to create in 1910. The bright red house perched on top of the 85-foot high tower is just a piece of trickery to disguise the water tank, the actual 'House' being within the superstructure below. And out in Lincolnshire, opposite the church in Potterhanworth, is a real bruiser – an impressive and sensitive conversion that keeps all the integrity of the 1910 tower and its original purpose, even down to a faux depth gauge on the iron tank.

Once a windmill becomes redundant and its internal workings are removed, there are only really two options: a quiet life as a roofless shell, slowly decaying out in the fields, or a re-birth as

" I told you at the time to get one with a corridor "

a conversation-piece home. Some thoughtful conversions retain as many original features as possible, others less so, but I do like the integration of the old Slaughden windmill in Aldeburgh into a jolly seaside house, which marries the green mill cap with pink shutters and a fish weathervane.

Dismantled railway lines offered many possibilities for those looking for excuses to dress up in old stationmasters' uniforms and blow Acme Thunderer whistles. Many rural stations had accommodation anyway, but a sizable home was gained once the ticket office and waiting rooms were added. Signal boxes turned into greenhouses, platforms were perfect for raised garden patios. French Drove station on the now dismantled Spalding to March line in Cambridgeshire even has an original carriage awaiting restoration, pulled up at one of the platforms on the grassed-over track bed.

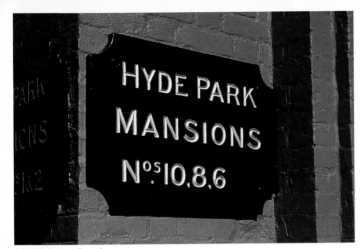

Marylebone, London

Hartley, Kent

Romsey, Hampshire

Chipping Campden, Gloucestershire

Cockersands, Lancashire

Birmingham

Thorpe Langton, Leicestershire

Spitalfields, London

Bournville, Birmingham

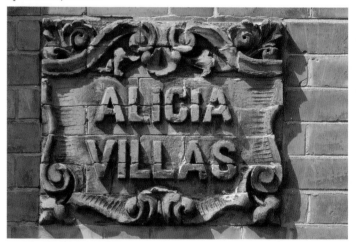

Clarendon Park, Leicester

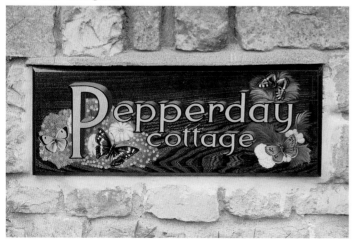

Barrowden, Rutland

Waterloo, London

THE GHOSTS OF CHRISTMAS PAST

After breakfast they all put on hats and coats, and went out into the garden. Daddy,
Benny and Susan had sharp knives for cutting holly sprays. Peter and Ann were to set the cut sprays
neatly together on the grass, ready for taking indoors. Then they would all help in putting them up.
The Christmas Book, Enid Blyton

opposite
Detail from a Crawford
Tartan shortbread
advertisement, 1948

Let's start by us all calming down, stop worrying about where we're going to get the life-size plastic Tardis for George, whether we can get away with not inviting Aunt Agnes again for Christmas and whether six bottles of Warnincks Advocaat is going to be enough. Pull up a chair to the fire, pour out a sherry and split open the Terry's Chocolate Orange.

I am old fashioned enough to believe that 25 December is the time chosen by a shivering monk somewhere to celebrate the birth of Christ. But I think the time of year is more to do with a canny desire to either suppress, or at least not upset, the Yuletide festival celebrated by blue painted pagans. The same reasoning that lies behind most original English churches being placed on the mounds and meeting places of the older religion. The Three Wise Men probably didn't take their camels down sludgy lanes to get to a snow covered stable, but I do believe, as perhaps T.S. Eliot did in his poem 'Journey of the Magi', that they '… returned to [their] places, these Kingdoms, / But no longer at ease here, in the old dispensation, / With an alien people clutching their gods.'

All of which I can't imagine means a great deal to the office workers staggering about the streets on Christmas Eve with a flashing pair of plastic reindeer horns on their heads. We have sadly come a long way from the traditional thoughts and sentiments of Christmas Past, not just in a pious religious sense, but also in our succumbing to the intense pressures brought to us courtesy of the sheer naked greed of commerce. Of course that doesn't mean to say that I would ever refuse to accept Betjeman's 'hideous tie so kindly meant' or even an iPod Nano, but increasingly I look back at my own Christmas Pasts somewhat wistfully. That's all this chapter is really, a personal reminiscence of a time when Christmas arrived in the shops sometime at the beginning of December and the most adventurous a greetings card got was a picture of a stage coach pulling up at a brightly lit roadside inn, with a little bit of glitter stuck on it if you were lucky.

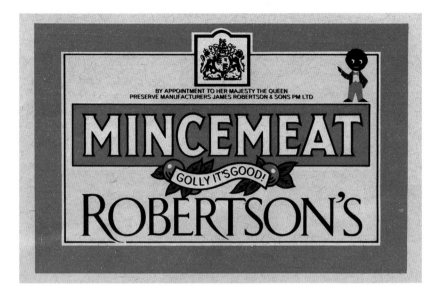

Early December

above left
Robertson's Mincemeat
label

above right
Boots the Chemist's
Christmas card, *c*. 1930

below
From Enid Blyton's
The Christmas Book,
the cliché of home for
Christmas from boarding
school. Illustration by
Treyer Evans

When I was a child in the 1950s the first hint of the approach of Christmas came with the Boots catalogue my father brought home in the evening. My mother and he had met whilst both were working at the Boots branch in Wellingborough in the 1920s, but once the liaison was discovered she was despatched without ceremony to the Matlock branch – I suppose just to make sure there were no 'goings on' behind the acid carboys and oxygen cylinders. (But at least she met Jesse Boot when he did a not very subtle 'secret shopper' act one foggy November afternoon.) Christmas shopping was therefore invariably accomplished by evenings of thumbing through the catalogue and turning down corners of the pages, followed by a visit to the Gallowtree Gate shop in Leicester clutching the staff discount card.

Of course there was the traditional writing out of the list to shove up the chimney for Santa Claus to act on, although my faith in this ordering system took something of a knock when I found one of my sooty lists stuck to a Brussels sprout stalk in the garden a few days later. But my mother did introduce me to Santa who for some reason was sitting in a plywood grotto in Lewis's department store. One year he memorably gave me a Wells Brimtoy clockwork bus after I'd mumbled in his ear for three minutes. When I got it home I pretended my thumb was a passenger and in sticking it up the tin stairs very nearly sliced it off on the razor-sharp tin. I think my father went and had words with the Lewis's management.

Maybe everyone was frenetically running about doing Christmas shopping and panicking

above, right and below
Christmas showcards from
Dudleys of Holloway, 1960

below right
Victorian Father
Christmas produced for
children's scrapbooks

about ordering pork pies, but I was blissfully
unaware of it. Santa arrived at Lewis's courtesy
of the Leicester Fire Brigade, who dragged him
around the streets sitting in a brightly lit sleigh
whilst firemen ran about in the crowds with
buckets. I think they still do something similar
in Hampton Hill in Middlesex, where Santa is
'rescued' from a rooftop with an escape ladder.
Apart from that I don't remember much else
going on to announce the season of goodwill
other than holly appearing around
advertisements in the evening newspaper
and the minister at our church announcing
Christmas services, which (inexplicably,
I thought) included one at midnight on
Christmas Eve. And of course there was more
of a thump on the mat as festive envelopes
started to drop from the letterbox.

H.M. The Queen
by St. John Ervine

Christmas Eve

The only real Christmas tree I saw was the one in Leicester's Town Hall Square. Ours was a little artificial one that came out (I think on Christmas Eve, certainly not much before) of a cardboard box with its flaps missing. The base was a wooden cube with Christmassy scenes pasted on and it was placed precariously on the sitting room windowsill. Later a string of coloured lights was added that swamped it completely and threatened to kill us all with its dodgy twists of flex. Not until Christmas Eve did I lie down on the rug in front of a banked-up coal fire with Enid Blyton's *Christmas Book* as the lane outside started to subside into darkness. I got up when I heard the clank of the lamplighter's ladder being put up to the lamp post to watch him turn up the greeny-yellow gaslight. (My own children think that this recollection is either me having caught false memory syndrome or just a downright lie, but it's true.)

The big brown wireless set was tuned into the Home Service (how cosy was that); after the valves had warmed through, carols from King's College, Cambridge filled the house (just as they still do); and the monotone *Radio Times*

Christmas Number was carefully consulted for the times of the 'Special Editions of all your favourite Variety Shows'. We had a little speaker rigged up on the kitchen wall, which connected with the master set so I could listen to *Children's Hour* whilst watching my mother doing something unpleasant to a chicken. By this time I was getting really excited at the prospect of Santa landing his sleigh in the divide between the twin gables of our house, and wondering whether he'd find the cricket ball I'd lodged up there in the summer. My excitement was tempered by threats from my two brothers that Santa would simply not arrive if they told him of my misdemeanours, however small. How this was to be accomplished I never asked; how I got to sleep I will never know. But I do know that one Christmas Eve I *did* hear sleigh bells descending from the frosty air above the house.

opposite
Card of Valentine's Christmas Gift Dressings

above left and centre
Christmas cards from a 1930s' scrapbook

above right
Homes and Gardens Christmas Number, 1945

Christmas Day

above
Robin, Holly, Mistletoe.
The ultimate Christmas
cliché we all love

First the slow dawning that this particular day was special; secondly the slow dawning that it was only half past three. But eventually it was time to negotiate the landing floorboards without setting foot on the loose one, and to see the bulging pillowcases tied to the wooden rails of the banister. The fact that nothing bore any resemblance to the items on my sooty lists was entirely forgotten as I delved down into the white cotton recesses, drawing out one parcel after another, all of them seemingly wrapped in thin white paper with red and green holly on it. Everyone always talks about getting an orange in their stockings, but aside from the fact that I had no interest in stockings until I had my first girlfriend, I never saw an orange, not so much as a tangerine.

After breakfast, and after the obligatory pork pie – you can't live in Leicestershire and not eat at least six at Christmas –, the fire was lit in what we euphemistically called 'the Lounge'. This room was usually only frequented by myself, crashing about tunelessly on the family piano, and consisted of a particularly 1930s'-looking settee and two armchairs. Not used to a fire for most of the year, the chimney belched smoke back into the room and we all ran outside coughing. Once we'd mopped tears

from our streaming eyes we settled down to some more present unwrapping. One year I'd tentatively written to Santa about a red Dinky Supertoy car carrier and trailer, transport much needed for eight of my saloon cars. I'd taken the precaution of leaving a secondary (misspelled) note on my mother's dressing table. My father held out a brown paper parcel and I tore off the wrapping to find the trailer. My elder brother smugly told me that owing to shortages at the Grotto the transporter to tow it wouldn't be available until next year. For one second I believed him, until I opened a second brown paper parcel.

The Christmas Dinner was always a cockerel – I've never liked the expression 'and all the trimmings' because I've always thought it sounded like the meal was draped in narrow strips of coloured paper and tinfoil – accompanied by the rituals of adults pulling at

right
Presents of Christmas
Past, including a 1929
Tri-ang pedal car, and
the essential Christmas
morning firelighting kit

below
An image of that elusive
White Christmas

wishbones and children fighting over sixpences
from puddings. If my Uncle Ray was a guest,
there was the entertainment of him fastening his
serviette to his suit jacket with a big brass clip.
(There was also the diversion of going into the
cold garage and sitting on his pale green BSA
motorbike with its colourful Bantam on the
petrol tank.) One year we had the additional
spectacle of my cousin Michael, looking very
pale, mysteriously going round all day with an
enamel washing up bowl under his arm.

above
The Christmas coaching
inn stereotype. Notice
how everybody leaves all
their lights on

left
A Regency Christmas
involving an awful lot of
holly

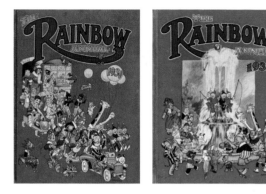

above

Christmas night bedtime
reading: the obligatory
annuals. *Rainbows* from
1930 and 1933

right

Something that goes bang
in the night. Firework
packet illustration *c.* 1930

Christmas Night

After struggling with Meccano (Dad: 'Just be patient boy') and playing out in the freezing cold hallway with a model battery-driven MG, the time came for Christmas Tea. More pork pie of course, and my father cursing under his breath at the bluntness of the ham knife and everyone going, 'Ooh look at that,' as the cake came out. But there was also something else that to this day I still don't fully understand or, indeed, have never had a meaningful conversation with anyone about. After all the paraphernalia of Tea had been cleared off the be-crumbed white tablecloth into the kitchen, we waited until my father appeared with a huge – well, to me it was – model of an ocean-going liner, which he placed as the centrepiece of the table like you would a flower arrangement. One year it was a lighthouse, but the effect was the same. The lights were turned out and we saw that the interior of the ship was lit up, yellow rays streaming out of cardboard cabin windows to reflect on our expectant – or, in my case, completely mystified – faces. Then, wait for it,

my father lit some kind of fuse. There was a brief fizz and a shower of sparks and then BANG, the whole thing exploded and showered us with sweets and cheap toys. It was a massive communal cracker going off in our faces; as far as I was concerned my father might as well have lobbed a hand grenade into the room. The lights went back on and blinking back to reality we all clapped as Dad lit a Player's up from the stub end of the fuse. Then it was either Hunt the Toffee, which was always behind my father's ear, or Crow Shoot, a game where we shot plastic crows off a wire with a cork-firing popgun. Bed came as quite a relief.

Boxing Day

above

A wonderfully graphic illustration of a jovial huntsman with his churchwarden clay pipe and top hat, from a 1930s' greetings card

The next day, St Stephen's Day if you're ecclesiastically minded, was very different. First the slow dawning that it wasn't Christmas Day, and that the next Christmas Day was in fact rather a long way off. After breakfast we'd watch Uncle Ray kick-start the BSA, his big goggles and leather helmet making us think he was about to do an Isle of Man TT Race, and after we'd wrestled the washing up bowl off Cousin Michael we probably just stared at each other or retreated to different parts of the house to read new books or, in my case, have another go at the Meccano. But one Boxing Day always stays pinned up on my memory board.

The Leicestershire countryside was designed for foxhunting, or at least it was in the late eighteenth and early nineteenth centuries. Fox coverts appeared on hillsides with names like Botany Bay, to remind the local populace about how easy it was to get transported to Australia, and Crackbottle, to remind everybody of the evening pleasures that lay ahead. Rolling hills, enclosed pastureland, hidden lodges and steeples to guide the chase.

Up until this Boxing Day, my experience of anything connected to foxhunting was severely restricted to Christmas cards with hounds in full cry across snowy countryside, and the red jackets and gilt riding crops on the blue covers of the Jorrocks editions of Surtees's books. But this was only because I'd never really been out into proper countryside on a deep midwinter morning before. This particular year the family's aspirations were suddenly realised in a car, my elder brother's battleship-grey 1939 Standard Eight. He was very keen that we should go and take a look at the Fernie Hunt's Boxing Day Meet in Great Bowden, where their hunt kennels are still tucked away in a little lane. So, sliding about on the blue leather seats the male contingent of the household set off for High Leicestershire to follow the chase. I think my other brother may have blown a horn out of the window.

above left
A Christmas walk in the woods. Members of my mother's family up in the Chilterns

above right
Advertisement for the Morris Oxford, 1951

below
John Minton drawing for 'The Great Snow' from H.E. Bates's *The Country Heart*, 1949

I don't remember much of the chase itself beyond a row of pink and black hunting coats on horses, lined up against the skyline. But I will never forget the first sight I had of the countryside we motored through. The winter morning was an English classic. A deep hoar frost encased every branch and twig in a glacial coating, the white fields striated with the lines of sheep walks, the breath from cattle in Welland Valley farmyards billowing out in clouds. All lit by a bright, low sun that would turn to a blood orange as the evening approached. And then I noticed the names of the villages: Glooston, Cranoe, Slawston. Names sounding like a perfect roll call for a winter's day. I just wanted to get out of the car and roll down a hillside, ruining my navy blue gabardine school mac. From that morning on I have not been able to hear those words from *The Holly and The Ivy* carol without thinking of this day; a door slowly opening for me: 'O the rising of the sun / And the running of the deer / The playing of the merry organ / Sweet singing in the choir.' Oddly, these words are written as I look out on precisely that same countryside, where I have very recently made my home after wandering about all over England, the pastures and woods now in shades of green and bathed in late afternoon summer light.

overleaf
A selection of the author's paintings of subjects local to his home, sent as greetings cards to family and friends for Christmas

Unforgettable Christmas

above
Keeping it simple.
Woodcut for a child's text
card from the 1920s

opposite
Weldon, Northamptonshire
with its cupola lantern
paid for by a traveller lost
in the Rockingham Forest,
in gratitude for the church
tower guiding his way

Childhood Christmases will resonate down the years with memories for all of us. We will always remember other high spots too, like the story of a friend's unforgettable Christmas when he was entrusted to remove the giblets bag from the Christmas poultry. For some reason he made sure of its detachment from the carcass with a marker pen which he proceeded to forget and leave inside the fleshy cavity. The expectant family watched in horror as a bright blue turkey was pulled out from the oven.

We once had the novelty, for us, of an oven with a timer. So, one Christmas we thought it would be a good idea to do something 'a little bit special' with it – we put a turkey in the oven, timed to cook for about six o'clock in the evening. And then we raced off across the Fens to the North Norfolk coast armed with a side of smoked salmon and a few bottles of fizz. I think some whisky was involved at Cousin Michael's (no washing up bowl in evidence), but we managed to get back home safely and on time, to the smell of a roasting bird. A bird the children had to sniff through the letterbox because we'd deposited the house keys on the beach somewhere near Cley-next-the-Sea. We did all sit down to eat our dinner, but only after I'd smashed through the front door glass with a wheel brace.

If you are fortunate, as I have been, to have the love and security of family life around you, all Christmases will be memorable. Particularly if one can resist, to a degree, the surge of commercial pressure and the mania of a build-up that now starts in September. And perhaps, if we can, look past the sentiment and those tissued fripperies to see the truth so ably expressed by John Betjeman in his poem 'Christmas':

No love that in a family dwells,
No carolling in frosty air,
Nor all the steeple-shaking bells
Can with this single Truth compare-
That God was Man in Palestine
And lives today in Bread and Wine.

ROLL OUT THE BARREL

They sell good Beer at Haslemere
And under Guildford Hill.
At Little Cowfold as I've been told,
A beggar may drink his fill:

There is a good brew in Amberley too,
And by the bridge also;
But the swipes they take in at Washington Inn
Is the very best Beer I know.

'West Sussex Drinking Song', *Hilaire Belloc*

opposite
Say, for what were
hop-yards meant,
Or why was Burton built
on Trent?
('A Shropshire Lad', A.E.
Houseman). Detail from
a Marston's Burton Bitter
beer mat

Beer was once as local as the nearest church. In fact, outside of castle and monastic brewhouses that was precisely where it all started, as ale was brewed and stored under the watchful eye of the priest in the church house, finally emerging for liberal consumption on feast days. Many church houses became inns, often retaining the name 'Church House Inn'. Indeed even if the name didn't survive, the proximity of so many village pubs to churches is remarkable.

As the process of brewing evolved it was just as likely that a local farmer would capitalise on having the basic ingredients immediately at hand, and the legend 'maltster and brewer' was added to the lettering on his farm wagons. But the eighteenth century saw the emergence of the brewery as we would recognise one today; Georgian structures that were subsequently replaced by substantial Victorian rebuilds designed to meet the voracious demands of a rapidly increasing population. William Bradford became their niche architect as breweries were built several storeys high to facilitate gravity-fed production, town church spires vying for attention with high water tank towers also

topped out with weather vanes and flagpoles.

Modern production methods now mean that local breweries can share their beers, ales and stouts with consumers far from their traditional bases, and the advent of the micro-brewery means we can enjoy guest bitters with doubtful names like Goblin's Knob in our local. But this chapter looks at the surviving breweries that, whilst achieving national distribution, have nevertheless maintained a presence either through their own pubs and hotels, or as a considerable local employer. It will be about true survivors; those breweries that have thus far steadfastly staved off the predations of competitors more interested in shareholder dividends. I dedicate it to the memory of Ridley's, the vanished Essex brewer with a remote rural brewery and an estate of eclectic pubs, downed in one gulp by Greene King.

Adnams

above
Postcards of Christopher
Wormell's illustrations
for Adnams Beer from
The Coast advertising
campaign

opposite
Bottle label for Adnams
Strong Suffolk Ale

below right
The ubiquitous bottle cap

Asked to sum up the East Suffolk coast of the past, one would probably think of Benjamin Britten, Adnams ale and sou-westered fishermen. Now it would be Benjamin Britten, Adnams ale and a sou-westered fisherman. Not a lot changes here, the Triumph Renowns arriving at Aldeburgh golf course replaced by Volvo 4x4s, the original tongue and groove boarding in the cottages painted in Farrow & Ball's Print Room Yellow. But Adnams in Southwold is still as local as a mackerel smoked in Orford, even though you can probably buy a bottle of it in Walsall.

Adnams really can claim a long pedigree in the town: their flagship hotel The Swan had a brewhouse out at the back six hundred and fifty years ago. But it wasn't until 1872 that Ernest and George Adnam bought the Sole Bay Brewery. George's interest in brewing waned and he disappeared off to Africa where he was promptly eaten by a crocodile, but Ernest

soldiered on and the tall brick brewery that rises over the pantiled rooftops was built in 1890.

Adnams dominates Southwold as much as the lighthouse that sends its beam out over Sole Bay. It keeps good local pubs and dray horses still help to deliver the ale to those not too far away. And a very promising sign of Adnams continuing success as both a local and now national brewer is the simple fact that brand new state-of-the-art brewing equipment was installed within the fabric of the Victorian brewery.

above and opposite, top
Hall & Woodhouse's
Blandford Forum brewery,
Dorset

opposite, bottom
Contemporary beer bottle
label for Badger Golden
Glory

left
Badger beer bottle labels
from the late 1970s

Hall & Woodhouse

Come over the hill to Blandford Forum from
Winterbourne Stickland on the top road and
you'll see the red brick brewery buildings of
Hall & Woodhouse dominating the scene
below. So obviously at the heart of its
community, this Dorset brewer can trace its
origins back to 1777 when Charles Hall, son of
a Dewlish farmer, maltster and brewer, founded
the Ansty Brewery. Within two years he had a
lucrative contract to supply troops lining up at
Weymouth to take on Napoleon. Charles's son
Robert expanded the business and by 1838 the
workforce included Edward Woodhouse, who
did the right thing by marrying Robert's niece
Hannah. Pole position on the wedding gifts

table was a partnership for Edward in the
brewery; and Hall & Woodhouse was born.

1936 saw Hall & Woodhouse becoming the
first brewer to start putting Best Bitter in cans.
Imagine that, the start of a lineage that would
stretch to the undersides of park benches the
whole world over. But this most local of local
brewers continued to deliver the barrels in
hand-cranked motor lorries that sported 'Beer is
Best' in metal letters on their tall radiator grilles.

These days you are more likely to recognise
the brand by the name Badger, and it's Badger
Blandford Fly you'll find in Iwerne Minster,
Golden Glory in Bishops Caundle and Tangle
Foot in Lytchett Matravers. Even local Hugh
Fearnley-Whittingstall picks nettles at his River
Cottage HQ for a summer thirst quencher
called Stinger.

Hook Norton

Farmer and maltster John Harris started brewing beer on the northern side of the Cotswolds in the mid-nineteenth century. His great great grandson James Clarke still runs what is one of only a handful of independent family brewers in the country. Once again it is a William Bradford Gothic pile that greets the visitor down a Hook Norton cul-de-sac, the sort of brewery that one would expect to be servicing Gormenghast. Bradford put everything in here: brick, slate, iron, weatherboarding and ironstone quarried from Hook Norton workings. He always wanted his breweries to look like glorious manifestations of the Industrial Age. Most brewery designs, he said, look like they were 'entrusted to the hands of the same gentleman who provides and fits up the pipes and cocks.'

The Hook Norton brewery produces an impressive range of beers – everything from high summer brews to black winter stouts –, some of it delivered locally on a dray pulled by shire horses with the evocative heavyweight names Consul, Major and Nelson. But for me the most startling thing is the horsepower gently hissing on the ground floor of the brewery. Hook Norton is probably unique in still using steam to pump wort, crush grain and

opposite
William Bradford's
towering brewery
buildings in Hook Norton,
Oxfordshire

right
Steam power at the Hook
Norton brewery

far right
Ceramic jug with the
classic Victorian image of
the brewery

power hoists. A 25 hp engine with a 7-foot
diameter flywheel is the iron heart at the centre
of operations. Starting work in 1899 it cost
£175. Not a bad investment really.

I wonder if they talk about 'water' when
discussing its mechanisms. One of the facts I
learnt very early on from a girl in a brewery was
that one never, ever, says 'water' when one's on
the premises. It's always 'liquor' in a brewery,
which is as it should be.

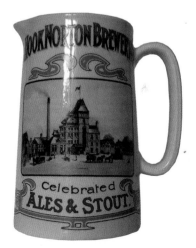

Harveys

above left
Enamelled sign outside
The Elephants Head,
Hook Green, Kent

above right
Harveys Bridge Wharf
brewery depicted in an
earlier age. This time-
honoured piece of sales
promotion was awarded
'Beer Mat of the Year' in
1990 by the British Beer
Mat Collectors Society

opposite
The Lewes brewery today

Harveys have no desire to be a national brewer. It suits them to serve a local area and have a portfolio of good pubs within a confined radius. Although I'm personally extremely grateful that their Sussex Bitter manages to get as far as Southwark, south of London Bridge. Seven generations of the Harvey family have brought liquors of all varieties to Sussex since the eighteenth century, but it was John Harvey who established the brewery in Lewes in 1790. In 1880 the Georgian buildings were enlarged by *über* brewery architect William Bradford, bringing Victorian Gothic to the banks of the River Ouse. At the topping-out ceremony in 1882 Bradford, the brewer and the contractor climbed up the chimney and christened the iron cap.

A contemporary report states that 'bumpers of champagne were drunk'. (Hopefully after their descent.) The whole site was put out of action for nine days in 2000 when the river rose up and flooded this part of Lewes, probably the first time that the rest of the country realised there was a brewery in the town. That's how Harveys like it, to be left alone to get on with brewing ales and porters for the cognoscenti and supplying their neighbourly pubs.

SUNLIGHT ON THE MECCANO

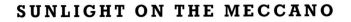

Well cut Windsmoor flapping lightly / Jacqmar scarf of mauve and green
Hiding hair which, Friday nightly / Delicately drowns in Drene;
Fair Elaine the bobby-soxer, / Fresh-complexioned with Innoxa…
'Middlesex', John Betjeman

opposite
In 1908 John Nichols
invented a medicine that
gave its takers 'vim' (to be
full of life); a vim tonic in
fact. Vimto was born, the
essential bubbles being
added in 1920

Seeing brand names in literature has always brought a sense of realism to the printed page. The everyday colliding with the exotic, as practised by Ian Fleming in his James Bond novels – Beefeater gin in *The Man with the Golden Gun*, Player's cigarettes in *Thunderball*. And, of course, Len Deighton's nameless anti-hero chuffing his way through the early novels with blue paper packets of Gauloises. Now it's unsubtly called 'product placement' and whole books are shamelessly written to tout consumer goods. But good old-fashioned brand names still have the power to move us in mysterious ways. Look how we all metaphorically marched on the Houses of Parliament, waving HP Sauce bottles, when Heinz shifted production to the Netherlands, for God's sake, after over a hundred saucy years in Birmingham. They might as well call it Van der Valk's Sauce and be done with it. The thing is we didn't even need to have been regularly chucking it over our chips to feel outraged by the decision. Along with millions of others I saw my first French words on the HP Sauce bottle – John Junkin wrote the lyrics for a song, *La Sauce HP*, which kicks off with the memorable line from the label: 'Cette sauce de haute qualité… ' – and one of my favourite actors, Dinsdale Landen, wrote a

whole book about it with his wife Jennifer Daniel, *The True Story of HP Sauce*.

Now I have to scurry off down to the shops every couple of months because I've heard on the news that KitKats are no longer to be wrapped in shiny foil, or that Smarties are going to be in stupid hexagonal cartons without the coloured plastic caps to push into bike spokes. (Actually I never understood that.) It's all getting out of control as my home fills up with Ovaltine tins with the Dairy Maid still on them and I spend the gas money on old Churchman's cigarette packets without the health warnings.

I blame my mother, of course. Our staple groceries were delivered on a Tuesday in a big maroon Morris van driven by a one-eyed man who frightened me by marching into the kitchen with a big wicker basket that he slammed down on the table. As a consolation for this rude interruption I was allowed to unpack and stare at each packet or box as it came out. The shot-putting man in a kilt on Scott's Porage Oats, Sifta Sam the jaunty sailor assuring me that his table salt was 'jolly good', the Op Art of the Oxydol soap powder box sending me cross-eyed…

above
Life after custard

top left
A post-war paper sachet
that made one pint of
custard

top right
Bird's trademark, first
used in 1929

right
Recipe book

Bird's Custard

I've always had a thing about custard. I think it's
because I was recognised by my school dinner
ladies as a likely receptacle for any spare custard
going at lunchtime. It was of a slightly insipid
variety, a pale, almost cream colour and came in
very 1960s' anodised metal jugs. I've also always
loved the word. Custard. It sounds tasty even if
you've never had it. And then of course there
was Bird's Custard, an essential addition to
spotted dick and treacle tarts, made from a
white powder. (How does it turn yellow?)

Bright yellow, a proper colour for custard,
although oddly there aren't any eggs used in its
manufacture. That's because Alfred Bird
experimented in 1837 with an eggless custard
to give to his young wife, who had what we
would call today 'allergies' – an intolerance, in
her case, to eggs and yeast-based products such
as bread. Apparently Alfred's custard got served
up at a dinner party by happy accident and,
such was the acclaim from his guests, the host
put it into production alongside his baking
powders. Coincidentally, he sold his products in
the same street in Birmingham, Bull Street, that
saw the birth of Cadbury's. (Another
Birmingham entrepreneur, Charles Dunlop,
provided some of his first pneumatic tyres for
Alfred's son's penny-farthing bicycle.)

above

Illustrations from
1940s' Bird's Custard
advertisements

The first advertisements appeared in 1880, with adaptations of traditional nursery rhymes like: 'When the pie was opened the birds began to sing the praises of Bird's Custard.' But the trademark of the three, slightly odd cut-out birds didn't flee the nest until 1929.

Every time I look at a tin of Bird's Custard these days it seems to be made by a different manufacturer, just another name in a 'brand portfolio'. The latest appears to be the excitingly named Premier Ambient Products, stuck out as it is on the Lincolnshire Fens near The Wash. But at least the evocative tricolour of the packaging has survived the countless changes over the years, even to the degree that the latest tins list the colours as one of the trademarks. And there's a Bird's 'Careline' you can ring if you're feeling a bit down and want to talk about custard.

above
Bovril promotion from the
First World War

right
Bovril were quite rightly
never afraid of declaring
the origins of their
product. A small space
advertisement from 1905

Bovril

Hot comforting mugs clasped by children's snow-caked gloves in Aga-warmed kitchens. Staple of the steamy bus garage canteen. Essential item ticked off the packing lists for balloonists' hampers. Even Captain Scott, iced up on a polar expedition in 1904, found time to write: 'The Bovril used on board the *Discovery* gave every satisfaction. It was especially useful with the cooking of seal meat.'

Bovril started out in the Canadian province of Quebec in 1874 as Johnston's Fluid Beef, the result of Scotsman John Lawson Johnston's experiments with canned meats to sustain French forts during the Franco-Prussian War three years earlier. But it wasn't until Johnston started production at 10 Trinity Square, London that the term 'Bovril' was coined for the dark meaty extract. The first recorded sales were in 1886, the *Colonial and Continental Exhibition* in South Kensington being used for

Who said BOVRIL?

above
Bristol Pottery mug

above right
Will Owen's 1925 poster

right
One of the most famous
Bovril posters, designed
by H.H. Harris in 1920.
The slogan was written
some time before, but
was withheld on news of
the *Titanic* disaster

free public tastings. The name links 'Bovine'
(cattle) with 'Vril' from Vrilya, a name used for
'life force' in Bulwer Lytton's novel *The Coming
Race*. Thankfully they don't feel they have to put
all that on the label.

The product shared its infancy with that of
commercial advertising, and Bovril were at the
forefront in producing innovative press and
poster campaigns. An early employee, Samuel
Benson, left in 1893 to establish himself as an
'advertiser's agent', with Bovril as his first
account. It turned out to be one of the longest
and most fruitful client-agency relationships
in history. Railway station enamel signs,
ceramic mugs and classic colourful posters
proudly brandished the logo, and John
O'Groats-to-Lands End walkers were soon
training only on Bovril.

My first encounter with Bovril came at an
open-air swimming pool in suburban Leicester,
in celebration of my not drowning. It was served
in the obligatory white mug in a kiosk that was
once, incredibly, the Purser's office from the
Mauretania, an ocean liner broken up in 1935.

Cadbury's

Quaker John Cadbury started it all in 1824, dealing in tea and coffee at 93 Bull Street in Birmingham. He attracted customers into the shop by having a 'real, live Chinaman' in native costume behind the counter. In his spare time Cadbury experimented in grinding cocoa beans and, by 1831, he was producing chocolate in a warehouse in Crooked Lane to be sold in his shop, incidentally the first in Birmingham to use plate glass in the windows. Cadbury's chocolate had finally arrived.

By 1879 the business had thrived to such a degree that work was started on a new factory 4 miles south of Birmingham. Surrounded by woods and fields and with the advantage of access by both rail and canal, Bournville (named by partners Richard and George Cadbury after the local Bourn stream) was an ideal location. In September of the same year the first trainload of girls and men arrived for work in what must have seemed a rural Elysium by comparison with their old workplace.

above
Award yourself the CDM. A Cadbury's promotion involving a tin medal

top
Cadbury's posters from 1931

right
Cadbury's deliveryman from the 1920s

Less than twenty years later, 300 acres on each side of the Bourn was acquired for the first houses of the Bournville Estate; an enterprise that grew into tree-lined streets surrounding what became known as the 'The Factory in a Garden'. The green spaces were put to use for recreation and George Cadbury encouraged his tenants to grow their own vegetables in their Arts and Crafts inspired houses and cottages.

Like Lever at Port Sunlight, he recognised that social evils came out of the bad housing conditions that workers had to endure, and knew that 'material and spiritual advantages' could be gained in a more rural environment. But in case anyone should think that all this was just Quaker altruism to keep the workers in order, a good percentage of the housing was put up for sale to those not involved in making bars of Cadbury's Dairy Milk at all, albeit under the watchful eye of the Bournville Trust. Come here on a late April day when the streets of red brick and half-timbered houses and bungalows are blessed with blossoming trees, come here at anytime and catch that unmistakable whiff of chocolate on the air.

above
1929 booklet given out to visitors to the Bournville Works

top right
Postcard of rhythmic dancing by Bournville employees

bottom right
Wrapper for wartime ration chocolate

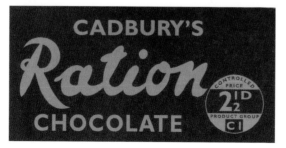

HP Sauce

above left
Dinsdale Landen and
Jennifer Daniel's HP
history book, using a
brilliantly executed
pastiche of an early label

above right
The classic bottle before
a succession of brand
managers got their hands
on it

below
Advertisement for
HP Sauce in *Good
Housekeeping* magazine,
February 1954

This is how I want to remember HP Sauce (see
the introduction to this chapter). A slightly
austere bottle with a monochrome photograph
of the Houses of Parliament on it. What an
endorsement. I really believed that the prime
minister tapped the brown condiment out over
his Monday morning cold mutton just like I did.
And if you'd been presented with cold mutton
on an equally cold Monday morning with wet
washing hanging over your head, you'd have
reached for the bottle too.

The foundation of a Wesleyan chapel
football club and the start of Edwin Samson
Moore's Midland Vinegar Company were the
two major events of the early 1870s that put
Aston in Birmingham on both the soccer and
condiment maps of England. When chips
arrived from France as an accompaniment to
fried fish, Moore of course insisted that vat loads
of vinegar would further enhance their flavours.

But he still hankered after making a table
sauce that would become a household name.
After much stirring and spooning he suddenly
found what he was after – a piquant sauce
brewing away in a washhouse copper
belonging to Mr Garton, a local grocer
indebted to Moore. Not only that, but the
name hastily written on a basket cart nearby
was Garton's HP Sauce. Garton explained that
he thought he'd probably heard a rumour that
his sauce might have nearly been seen in the
Houses of Parliament. It must have been one
of the quickest and vaguest sales pitches in
history. Garton's debt was cancelled and recipe
and name bought for £150. His name didn't
leave the label of Garton's HP Sauce until food
rationing commenced in 1940. And, at the
time of its dismal departure to the land of the
polder, HP Sauce in Aston had survived twenty-
two prime ministers.

improves all meals

Spratt's

above left
An extinct brand that managed to express itself with wit, character and great graphic style. A rarity indeed

above right
One of Corgi's re-runs of famous Dinky Supertoy van liveries

James Spratt arrived in England from Cincinnati, Ohio. His original intention had been to sell lightening conductors (just ahead of thunder storms perhaps) but his attention was oddly distracted by dogs on London quaysides snuffling around for stray ships' biscuits. His dog 'cakes' were launched in 1890, but by the 1930s Spratt's products were introduced for other household pets, each with its own calligram – a graphic device that combines a concept with a word and picture. The most famous is of course the Spratt's dog, a Scottie drawn to such simple stunning effect by Max Field-Bush. There were also calligrams for cats, birds and fish.

I first saw the Spratt's dog on a Dinky Supertoys Guy van, bought for me by an adoring aunt in Skegness. It went missing fairly early on, so now I have only the Corgi *homage* to stare at, but nevertheless I thought the dog wagging his tail was just the cleverest thing I'd ever seen. In their essential little black book, *Logo R.I.P.*, The Stone Twins say of all the calligrams, 'they were an instant success and have character, wit and graphic strength that is rarely seen today.'

Port Sunlight

above and opposite
Magazine inserts
advertising Port Sunlight
products

right
The bright primary-
coloured packaging for
two bars of Sunlight Soap

When William Hesketh Lever was on holiday
on one of his favourite Scottish islands, he was
suddenly seized with the idea of abandoning
his father's hugely successful grocery business
and trying his hand at making soap. Nobody
knows why – perhaps it was something to do
with a virulent stain he'd got on his trousers –,
but on 27 October 1885 a chemical works he'd
leased in Warrington saw the first boiling up of
his new soap. In the previous year he had
registered the brand, and so excited was he –
and so worried someone else might get there
first –, that he probably ran to the registration
office with the name Sunlight. Once the soap

below right
Will Owen and other
designers brought
paternal village ideals to
Lord Leverhulme's Port
Sunlight on the Wirral in
Cheshire

had slipped into the shops it quickly became a phenomenal success.

What followed was rapid expansion into a vast new works in Cheshire, an enterprise immediately christened Port Sunlight. But it wasn't just Sunlight, Lifebuoy, Persil, Lux or Vim that placed Lever's towering soaperies on the map. Lever, soon to be the first Lord Leverhulme, placed the welfare of his workers high on his list of nonconformist ideals. Three years after his arrival on the Wirral he began work on low-cost housing set in as natural an environment as possible; a far cry from the abysmal 'back-to-backs' experienced by contemporary workers in other industries. Here is an architectural landscape reliant on Arts and

Crafts features such as half-timbering and Dutch gables; red brick contrasting with green lawns, hedges and flowering shrubs. All impossibly bright and clean, as you would expect.

above
Cardboard cut-out
Robertson's Golly

right and below right
Paper token Gollies and
needle case

below
Footballing Golly enamel
badge, *c.* 1960, by
Fattorini, Birmingham

The Robertson's Golly

Has there ever been such a pitifully and wrongly maligned character from the world of brand characters? The red-trousered, blue-jacketed Golly helped Robertson's sell forty-five million jars of their products every year. And how many complaints did they have each year about using a child's toy to promote their brand? Ten, if they were lucky.

The Golly motifs lasted ninety-one years before the last enamel brooch was sent out on 11 November 2002. In that time the character was printed on labels, mugs, teapots, toast racks, made into collectors' badges, moulded into figurines and inflated into hot air balloons. The best piece of Golly merchandising I ever saw was

a wooden shop display figure, about 3 feet high, which held a real jar of Golden Shed in a gloved hand, illuminated by a light bulb from behind.

The Golly was replaced by characters from Roald Dahl books but, amazing though they are, Quentin Blake's illustrations simply do not translate into badges. They were discontinued after three years. The dead hand of marketing you see. Nothing can be permanent anymore; nothing can be timeless. As if to prove the point, at the same time as the Golly got kicked into touch, Robertson's launched a new range of jams and marmalade called Absofruitly. But on a more heartening note, there appears to more interest in collecting Robertson's Gollies now then ever there was when they had jobs in advertising.

The Bisto Kids

The origin of the word Bisto is one that has a hint of post-rationalisation about it. Very like 'Odeon' being thought of as 'Oscar Deutsch Entertains Our Nation', Bisto was apparently derived from the initial letters of 'Browns, Seasons, Thickens In One', and was then rearranged a bit.

The Cerebos company introduced Bisto in 1908: a meat-flavoured powder that could be added to a cook's own gravy. In 1919 Will Owen – who did one of the Bovril posters on page 111 – drew the poster of a ragamuffin boy and girl blissfully sniffing a waft of gravy and going 'Ah!'. They quickly became synonymous with the brand, and Bisto's subsequent popularity is astounding. In marketing speak it is one of those iconic brands that enjoys 100% distribution, which means that you're almost guaranteed to find it in every grocer's shop in the country. But the 'Ah!' is all that survives (albeit extended to 'Aah!'), the Bisto Kids having been dropped some time ago, presumably put into the Home for Old Advertising People (OAPs) along with Fry's Five Boys and the beautiful succession of Ovaltine Dairy Maids. And, of course, our friend opposite.

above
Catering-size Bisto tin

above right
Will Owen's Bisto Kids

right
Bisto press advertisement, December 1943

RICH THICK GRAVY HELPS THE KITCHEN FRONT

Meccano

above
A helicopter built with
Meccano Outfit No. 5
(clockwork motor not
included)

**opposite, clockwise
from top**
Instruction manual for
Outfit No. 3, which didn't
have all the parts for
this crane; the monthly
Meccano Magazine
that gave, amongst
many other things,
ideas for new models;
detail of a right-angle
drive mechanism and
a Meccano leaflet from
1954–55

below
Early Meccano model

In the superb television film *The Combination*, set in and around Church Stretton in the Shropshire of 1951, the actor Gary Raymond is seen having a 'nervous breakdown' (as we used to call it) in a garden shed. His anguish manifests itself through his total absorption in building something – we're not quite sure what – out of Plaster of Paris and red and green Meccano parts. I think this was the one and only time I'd ever seen anyone but myself attempt to construct anything from these intimidating pieces of metal and tiny nuts and bolts. Whether this surreal scene triggered the breakdown is not clear.

In the first years of the twentieth century Frank Hornby invented what was to become one of the most successful construction toys ever. The name Meccano soon became synonymous not just with perforated metal but also with Hornby trains and Dinky toys. In terms of quality and quantity, the decades from 1920 to 1940 were the original Meccano's finest hours, prompting a tradition that would see countless schoolboys struggling to fit pieces of green and red (sometimes yellow and blue) pieces of metal together with impossibly small brass nuts and bolts. Dining room tables became test beds for myriad permutations, everything from miniature swing boats to massively complicated gantry cranes. And you could build up your collection of bits and pieces in easy stages – a No. 1 set could be converted to a No. 2 with set No. 1a, and No. 2 to a No. 3 with a No. 2a, and so on. Right up to the grandiose and frightening No. 10, which came in a wooden box and meant you could rule the engineering universe. I didn't progress much beyond being able to make a little garden seat and a wheelbarrow. I fiddled about with some of the new stainless steel stuff a while back and found myself swearing quite unnecessarily, and I perhaps realised why this activity really should be confined to garden sheds.

MECCANO

Registered Trade Mark

INSTRUCTIONS for OUTFIT No. 3

COPYRIGHT BY MECCANO LIMITED
BINNS ROAD, LIVERPOOL 13, ENGLAND

53.3 *

W. H. PINYON.

The Toy of the Century

1954-5

MECCANO

MADE IN ENGLAND BY MECCANO LTD.

VOL. XLIV No.5   MAY 1959

MECCANO MAGAZINE

THE CALEDONIAN
46244

1/5

DOWN THE CUT

…the canals flowed clear and sparkling in the sunshine, something new in the landscape with their towpaths, lock-keepers' cottages, stables for canal horses…and (the) long and narrow gaily-painted boats.
The Making of the English Landscape, W.G. Hoskins

opposite
Detail from the poster for *Painted Boats*, 1945, an Ealing Studios film. The designer was John Piper, who thought he took the cartouche that surrounds the title from a rubbing he made of a Leicestershire gravestone

We didn't say 'cut' in our house. The 'cut' was where scruffy kids went angling for minnows and newts with jam jars and homemade fishing rods. We cycled along the 'canal' towpath with bottles of Vimto and bananas in our saddlebags, saying, 'Good morning,' to fishermen huddled over maggot tins who completely ignored us. The canal bank was a world we felt at home in. It wasn't a road where petrol tankers could force us into the kerb, it wasn't fields where irate farmers would go red-faced and shout, 'Get orf my laand you bleeders,' whilst gesturing with a horny finger. The very nature of the canal meant that the going was always level, the bridge 'holes' were exciting because there was always the chance of banging your head on the brickwork if you didn't dismount, and the locks were always there to beckon us to contemplate horrible death in their gloomy depths.

Although the Romans had a go at canal building and there's an Elizabethan bypass around weirs on the River Exe, the first proper canals arrived in England when James Brindley navigated a waterway in the 1760s to connect the Duke of Bridgewater's coalmines at Worsley with Manchester. These days saw the first belchings of smoke attendant on the Industrial Revolution, and the new furnaces and workshops now demanded fuel on a hitherto unimaginable scale, their products needing a faster distribution than pack horses lumbering on muddy roads for weeks on end could manage. It wasn't long before canal engineering brought bridges, locks, aqueducts and boatlifts. Wharfs and warehouses transformed villages and towns, and whole communities sprang up to serve the new navigations. That was, until a lone whistle sounded the first warning of cataclysmic change and gradual decline, the coming of the railway age.

But we can still enjoy over 2,000 miles of landscaped waterways that combine engineering with architecture, natural history with social history, and boating with walking and angling. The thundering rush of water in a lock, the rainbow flash of a kingfisher. And there's really nothing like sitting at the front of a narrow boat with a large bottle of beer in one's hand as the 'navigator' pilots the whole thing straight into the overhanging trees.

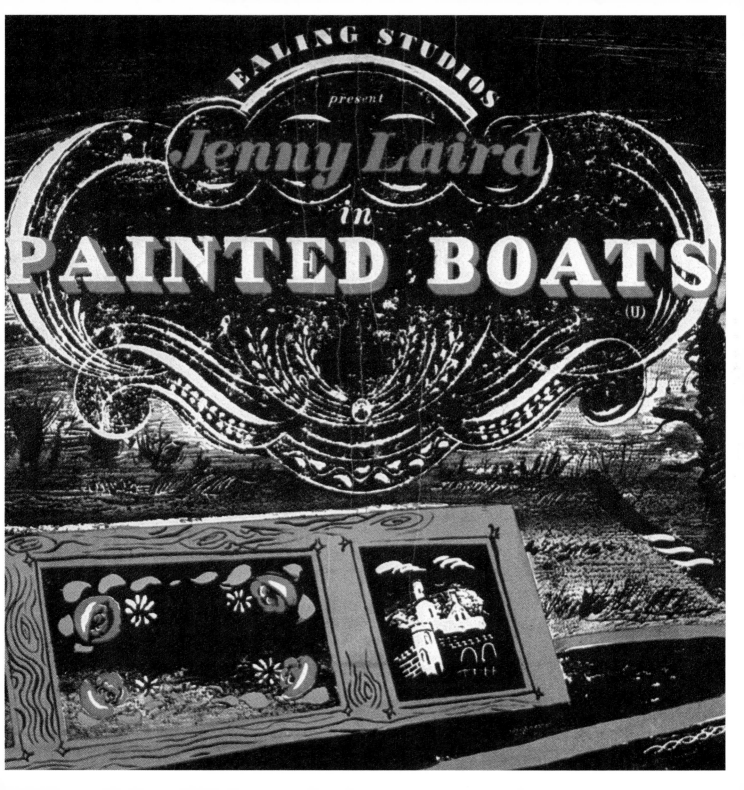

Landscape and Atmosphere

above
The cool of the evening
on the Ashby Canal
at Snarestone in
Leicestershire

Canals are the hidden waterways of the urban environment. Motionless behind high-walled factories where waste pipes gush out into the still water; surfaces mirroring traffic-laden iron bridges before widening out into basins where narrow boats can line up together in snug dependence. In London they fringe cemetery and industrial estate alike, but, equally, they can be both the tree-lined channels hiding at the back of cream stucco Regency villas, or the *russe in urbe* views seen from the high windows of red brick mansion blocks.

But the winding course of a canal in the countryside is likely to be our most popular remembered image of man-made waterways. The Grand Union making its way through quiet Midland pastures, the green of trees and hedgerows contrasting with the orange bricks of the accommodation bridges, and the engineering blues of lock chambers. The Trent & Mersey avoiding Nottingham and Derby until fetching up amongst Burton beer barrels and Staffordshire Potteries. Out on the Shropshire Union, with A.E. Housman's 'blue remembered hills' always on the horizon, Dutch-style white painted lift bridges pulled up against dark oaks. Grey northern granites outline tunnel entrances and wharves on the Huddersfield

above
The grip of winter on the Grand Union Canal at Foxton in Leicestershire

above right
Wood engraving of a typical canal scene by George Mackley

right
Tunnel of greenery on the Harborough Arm of the Grand Union.

Narrow and the Leeds and Liverpool Canals, classical lodges mark the progression of the airy Gloucester & Sharpness Canal, power stations reflect in the broad reaches of the Aire & Calder Navigation. All punctuated by black and white painted mooring bollards, lock gates and cast-iron mileage signs. But that's for the survivors; many canals have simply gone to ground, leaving only the occasional reed bed or furrowed field to mark their passing.

Lock and Cottage

above and below
Foxton Locks,
Leicestershire

Canals are not rivers. They were quite literally cut out of the landscape – hence 'The Cut' – and, until the introduction of locks, they followed the land's natural contours in circuitous routes. Probably the best place to get to grips with how the lock system works is to

follow a boat on its journey up or down the staircase of locks at Foxton in Leicestershire. Here, five pairs of locks descend 75 feet to the start of High Leicestershire, where boats have a choice of taking the 6-mile arm that curves around Gallow Hill to the Market Harborough basin or the main route to the Saddington Tunnel and Leicester.

Where there are locks there will often be a lock-keeper's cottage. There aren't many lock-keepers these days, the job of opening sluices and pushing open the balance beams left to those navigating the boats. But they must be enchanting places to live, shades of *The Bargee* film with Harry H. Corbett and Ronnie Barker. I nearly lived in one once, but was dissuaded from the notion by loved ones who had visions of my forgetting where I lived and walking out at night straight into the lock.

All cottages on the canal, whether for lock- or bridge-keeping, come in a variety of shapes and materials. I particularly like the barrel-roofed dwelling at Lowsonford on the Stratford-upon-Avon Canal (see the photograph in the gallery on page 132) built with the curved former used in the construction of the neighbouring bridge, and the lengthsman's round house at Chalford on the overgrown Thames & Severn. Out on the airy Gloucester & Sharpness can be found little porticoed lodges for bridge-keepers with a classical sense of authority, probably sourced by the canal engineers from a pattern book of Toll Houses and Gate Lodges.

above left
Frampton-on-Severn, Gloucestershire

above right
Barge on the Grand Union Canal by Clarke Hutton, from *Popular English Art*, 1945

left
Chalford Round House, Gloucestershire

far left
Audlem, Cheshire

Bridge and Aqueduct

above left
Newton Harcourt,
Leicestershire

above right
Foxton, Leicestershire.
Weight limit sign
originally on the Oxford
Navigation

The experience of moving about the canals in boats, on foot or by bicycle, is always imbued with a sense of expectancy, particularly if one is travelling along an unfamiliar stretch of water. The canal is no motorway with giant blue signs telling you of everything ahead well in advance, and usually we can't see very far into the distance anyway. Our curiosity of what's around the next bend is usually satisfied by the sight of a lock heaving into view, but it could equally be a bridge – a brick, stone, iron or timber distraction from reed-lined water.

Sometimes it will be an 'accommodation' bridge, a brick arch built to accommodate local farmers in moving their stock or equipment from field to field. Look out for the grooves where the arch meets the towpath, gouged over decades by the ropes of horse-drawn barges. Bridges can equally be graceful sweeps of iron with founders' names cast into their parapets, and out on the Shropshire Union or Oxford Canals we are more likely to see white painted timber lift bridges with their balancing arms tilting up and down against the sky like something from a Dutch watercolour.

But for something really amazing, the Barton Aqueduct in Manchester takes some beating. Here the Bridgewater Canal crosses over the

right
Stone-built Solomon's Bridge, Cosgrove, Northamptonshire

far right
Cast iron in Braunston, Northamptonshire

below right
Barton Aqueduct, Manchester

below left
Timber Wrenbury Lift Bridge, Cheshire

Manchester Ship Canal on a single 234-foot span that contains 800 tons of water. If a ship approaches that needs the space, an operating tower on an island in mid-stream swings the sealed-off tank sideways. (There are two more pictures of it in the gallery of photographs on pages 132 and 133.) The hydraulic power silently moves 1,600 tons, which is a very Fred Dibnah kind of engineering marvel.

Barton Aqueduct, Manchester

Lowsonford, Warwickshire

Stoke Bruerne, Northamptonshire

Long Buckby, Northamptonshire

Hawkesbury Junction, Warwickshire

Bulbourne, Hertfordshire

Great Haywood, Staffordshire

Foxton, Leicestershire

Shardlow, Derbyshire

Stoke Bruerne, Northamptonshire

Sapperton Tunnel, Gloucestershire

Barton Aqueduct, Manchester

Castle and Rose

Many see the castles and roses painted on canal narrow boats as expressions of the colourful fantasies and dreams of homes so materially different from the cramped conditions of life on the canals; the roses metaphorically plucked from the gardens of lock-keepers' cottages to create painted gardens on everything from boat sides to coffee pots and Buckby cans. (These tin buckets are named after the little shop at Buckby Wharf where the boatman could buy his can in instalments, dropping off a few pennies every time he passed by.) Certainly the decorations are related to English popular arts, as seen at fairgrounds, on gypsy caravans and traditional farm wagons. They were predominately found on the narrow boats of independent owners, the 'Number Ones'. They must have provided welcome visual relief from the grim backgrounds of northern industry that were so often the all too real backdrop to daily life.

The truth is nobody really knows how these beautiful decorations evolved and they were frequently changed, perhaps as a result of the latest plate designs being seen as they were transported in cargoes from the Staffordshire Potteries, whereupon they were copied and passed on within the community. Tony Lewery in his *Signwritten Art* puts it very succinctly: 'In a proper example of a well-painted canal boat there is a very happy integration of romantic imagination with utility.'

Tunnel and Ventilator

above left
Standedge Tunnel, West
Yorkshire

above right
Blisworth Tunnel
Ventilator,
Northamptonshire

below
The horse path and
ventilator for the canal
tunnel at Braunston in
Northamptonshire

If, like me, you have a leaning towards the
slightly odd, then you won't be able to keep
away from canal tunnels. There is something
decidedly spooky about walking along a
towpath on a hot summer's day and coming
across the gaping black maw of a tunnel
opening. If you're on a boat then you brace
yourself for a dark, dripping and disorientating
experience; if you're walking then you have no
option but to take the old horse path over the
top, unless you want to swim down it Captain
Webb-style. But at least up here you will see the
stark ventilator chimneys out in the fields.

Working on building a tunnel was extremely
dangerous; men working in foul air by
candlelight, never knowing when their picks
might break through into wet sand or cause a fall
of earth and rock. Water had to be continually
pumped out, but once it was lined in brick or
stone people queued up to have their wits
frightened out of them on inaugural boat trips.

The Blisworth Tunnel is 3,056 yards of terror.
In the early nineteenth century a steam tug failed
to emerge at its appointed time, only to later
appear with the crew of two dead from
suffocation, thus hastening the arrival of
ventilators to cope with the exhaust of powered
craft. Near the southern portal is a little building
that was once the waiting room for 'leggers', who
took boats through by walking them with their
feet on the tunnel walls. Nearby also is Candle
Bridge where they bought their tallow dips.

Standedge Tunnel on the Huddersfield
Narrow Canal in West Yorkshire is the longest at
3 miles 135 yards. A rare treat down here was
once the close proximity of steam trains sharing
the same space for a moment, the two
navigations boring through Pennine granite
only separated by galleries, the acrid smoke
billowing out onto the canal. L.T.C. Rolt said of

above left
Tunnel House Inn, near
Coates, Gloucestershire

right
Sapperton Tunnel,
Coates, Gloucestershire

below
Saddington Tunnel,
Leicestershire

it: 'Altogether a closer approximation of the legendary route to the infernal regions by way of the Styx it would be difficult to conceive.'

The Sapperton Tunnel in Gloucestershire is positively horticultural by comparison, a surviving fragment of the Thames & Severn Canal, with its 1789 yellow Cotswold stone southern portal. This beautiful classical arch by Josiah Clowes sits surrounded by greenery and is almost in the garden of the Tunnel House Inn, originally built to house canal workers.

Wharf and Yard

above
Stourport, Worcestershire

right
Stoke Bruerne,
Northamptonshire

The business of canals operated between centres of trade and commerce, and also in the boatyards, where essential maintenance work could be carried out. Sadly, much of this has disappeared, with wharfside buildings being turned into waterside apartments and anything approaching an oily rag and a hefty spanner sent into exile so that workshops can be cleared away to make way for 'retail opportunities'. Real canal life is shunted out of sight so that menus in towpath pubs can tempt us – or not – with Bargee's Chilli Dips.

In 1772 all that stood at the confluence of the Severn and Stour was an alehouse. Bewdley was the favoured site for James Brindley to bring his Staffordshire & Worcestershire Canal into the Severn, but the townspeople feared a dramatic drop in their trade and so told him to take his 'stinking ditch' elsewhere. Brindley did precisely that, and the resulting complex of Georgian wharves and warehousing at Stourport promptly brought Bewdley to its Georgian knees.

L.T.C. Rolt talks fondly of the canal shop at Stoke Bruerne in his wonderfully evocative *Narrow Boat* (1944). Apart from coils of ropes and lines there was everything a boat family could need: crusty loaves, tea and jam, crockery, those fat earthenware teapots, hurricane lamps, saucepans and kettles. And the essentials – shag tobacco and gobstoppers for the children. Some of these things I'm sure you can still purchase at Stoke Bruerne, but one of the stone-built warehouses is now a fascinating canal museum.

above left and centre
Bulbourne, Hertfordshire

above right
Shardlow, Derbyshire

Faded crumbling lettering that once spelt out 'Stevens, Millers & Merchants' still speaks of past activity at Shardlow, an eighteenth-century inland port on the Trent & Mersey in Derbyshire. Hints of decaying grandeur, with the obviously domestic door fanlights used for warehouse windows. Perhaps leftovers from a boat consignment meant for the merchants' fine houses still to be found a discreet distance away from their businesses.

But however much the canals now serve as the backdrops to water-borne holidays, the matter of repairing the infrastructure still goes on. So, it was very gratifying to discover big blocks of woods for lock repairs stacked up in a yard at British Waterways' Bulbourne depot in Hertfordshire. Built in the 1890s for the Grand Junction Canal, a classic set of workshops are strung out between workers' cottages and the yard manager's house. The centrepiece is a Gothic tower doubtless designed to provide an eyrie to watch over all the activity below.

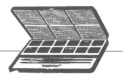

UMBRELLAS AND PAINT

'You've been pretty unlucky with the weather, Mr Piper.'
King George VI to John Piper

opposite
Rigby Graham
*Horkstow – George and
the Bluebottles* (detail),
1994, linocut

The English suffer for their art. Forget about running around going mad in the South of France and trying to blow your brains out in a cornfield, we sit about in the rain and catch colds. Or, if you're George Stubbs (pictured opposite in Rigby Graham's linocut), catch something much worse from the dead horses you've got strung up in your studio just so you can get the muscle tones right. Mr Graham himself is often to be found out in all weathers, setting up his paint-bespattered easel amidst dripping cow parsley on the roads of Leicestershire and Rutland. And I think this is what informs my preferences in English art, the ones that connect with the landscape in a way that I can understand and appreciate. Eric Ravilious's view of the Westbury White Horse from a third-class train compartment – I think to myself 'I've done that' (well, almost). And then John Piper's luminescent *Harlaxton Manor*, suddenly expressing how I feel about that massive pretend Elizabethan pile on its Lincolnshire hillside, an eerie madman's castle in the air. Even though these pictures may get finished off in a warm studio, you still know that the artists have been out there, stood about, taken snaps, made sketches, just stared at their subjects for a long time.

All kinds of threads and connections came together for me in April 1983. I wandered into the Hayward Gallery on London's South Bank – if one actually does wander into any building around there – and found myself in an exhibition. I nearly made an exhibition of myself as I was confronted by *Landscape in Britain 1850–1950*.

A hundred years of interpretations of what I loved best – the countryside that I worked in, travelled in, lived and loved in. Everything I could have wished for, from Joseph Southall's 1928 *The Botanists* (two girls wearing 1920s' hats in seductive poses on a cliff top) to Edward McKnight Kauffer's 1931 poster for *Stonehenge* (big abstracted megaliths on a starry night). Brian Cook originals for Batsford book covers, S.R. Badmin's original for his *Shropshire* Shell poster (pass me the smelling salts). I don't like to misuse the word epiphany, but I think I had one.

The Brothers Nash

Some of the most evocative images of the English countryside are perhaps seen in the work of Paul Nash (1889–1946) and his brother John (1893–1977). Both survived the horrors of the First World War; both were official War Artists who produced memorable pictures of subjects in both world wars. But they were firmly rooted in the tradition of English landscape painting, Paul finding great inspiration in the mystical work of William

Blake and Samuel Palmer, and John, much encouraged by his older brother, reflecting a gentler tempo of country life in his watercolours and wood engravings. John wrote that both he and Paul only worked for their own pleasure after six o'clock in the evening, when their war work was finished for the day. One has only to look at some of the paintings of this period to see long evening shadows reaching out over orchards and cornfields.

Paul was a pioneer of Modernism, his enthusiasms drawing him to abstraction and, in particular, surrealism. And where John's work is perhaps a thoughtful record of nature and the rural activity in and around it, Paul's visions lie much deeper in what he termed 'genus loci' or 'spirit of place'. Paul shocks his military superiors with an image of a broken-backed German plane under an English chalk cliff; John is content with showing us how a threshing machine works on an English summer's day.

Eric Ravilious

above
Eric Ravilious
Train Landscape, 1939

below
Eric Ravilious's *Alphabet* mug for Wedgwood, 1937. Ravilious placed 'Y' on the inside so that the yacht would appear to float on the beverage

Even if this slightly strange sounding name is not familiar, most of us will have seen the work of Eric Ravilious on the front cover of countless *Wisden Cricketers' Almanacks*. The engraving of a top-hatted batsman and wicket keeper has adorned the bright yellow covers since 1938, a constant in a changing age. If we're lucky we may also have seen one of his very desirable lithographs of shops from J.M. Richards's *High Street*.

Ravilious is also a tragic symbol of unfulfilled potential; a brilliant career as painter, muralist, designer of graphics and pottery, and wood engraver cut short when the Hudson air-sea

above
Engravings for the front covers of a series of Country Walks booklets published by London Transport, 1936

above right
Eric Ravilious *The Westbury Horse*, 1939

rescue plane he was flying in as a War Artist disappeared off Iceland in September 1942. But what a legacy he left for future generations to enjoy. The early work produced whilst sharing a house in Essex with fellow RCA student and great friend Edward Bawden – views from upstairs windows, bedrooms with patterned wallpaper, garden tables set for tea, abandoned farm implements on bleak downland.

And his fascination with chalk figures cut from those same slopes. The two paintings reproduced here always bring to mind Philip Larkin's lines in 'The Whitsun Weddings': '… none thought of… how their lives would all contain this hour.' The same moment caught in the two entirely different viewpoints of empty railway compartment and windy hillside.

Edward Bawden

above left
Edward Bawden
Ealing Studios poster for
The Titfield Thunderbolt,
1953

above right
Edward Bawden
Cover for *London
A-Z*,1953

below right
Edward Bawden
The Lion of England,
designed for the
coronation of Queen
Elizabeth II, 1953

Edward Bawden survived his friend Eric Ravilious by forty-six years, quietly getting on with his painting, drawing, engraving and printmaking in his Saffron Walden studio. But both came to prominence when they were chosen and commissioned to paint a mural for the Refreshment Room at Morley College in South London in 1928. It gave them instant success and recognition, setting the background for their working together, albeit on independent projects, until Ravilious's untimely death in 1942.

The influence each had on the other is easily seen, with Bawden's witty line drawings contrasting with Ravilious's tighter more disciplined style. Bawden's work was much in demand with publishers for book jackets, and his bright graphic work was much admired in

above
Edward Bawden
Cattle Market, Braintree,
1937. Lithograph from
linocut

right
Edward Bawden
Logo for the Provincial
Booksellers Fairs
Association, 1983

jobs for Fortnum & Mason and the London Underground. Anyone who has thumbed through an early Shell Guide will have seen his gently punning advertisements for the petrol company. In later years his printmaking was prolific; but I particularly like his *Cattle Market, Braintree,* a linocut made in 1937. The design elements are so strong, with almost repeat patterns occurring in the animal pens.

Charles Tunnicliffe

above
Charles Tunnicliffe
Images from the Ladybird
Book *What to Look for in
Autumn*

opposite
Charles Tunnicliffe
Cutting the Wheat, from
Both Sides of the Road,
1949

below right
Charles Tunnicliffe
Scraperboard from
Plowmen's Clocks, 1952

When the illustrated edition of Henry
Williamson's *Tarka the Otter* came out in 1932, the
illustrator was Charles Tunnicliffe. This first
commission set the seal of success on a career
that saw this Cheshire-born artist become one of
our best-loved depicters of the natural world,
particularly in his characterful paintings of birds.

I must have first come across his work in the
seasonal series he did for Ladybird Books – *What
to Look for in Spring*, followed by volumes for
Summer, *Autumn* and *Winter*. The text was by E.L.
Grant Watson, but the full-page illustrations were
Tunnicliffe's: deeply atmospheric scenes of
country life that completely captured my
imagination. A barn owl perching in the
moonlight amidst Traveller's-joy and a red-
berried wayfaring tree; a pale church tower rising
up above haystacks. A leather-jerkined, pipe-
smoking shepherd watching a skein of whooper
swans cross an autumn sky as he tends his sheep
near his blue painted mobile hut. Or swallows
gathering on lichened roof tiles in preparation
for their long-haul flights. All of these from just
one of the books, *What to Look for in Autumn*.

Later I kept coming across Tunnicliffe's
wood engravings and scraperboards, in books
like Alison Uttley's *Plowmen's Clocks* and Brian
Vesey-Fitzgerald's *Rivermouth*. But I think the
book that really set me back on my heels was
Both Sides of the Road, a brilliant collaboration
with Sidney Rogerson. Subtitled 'A Book about
Farming', his biographer Ian Niall has since
written about it:

*He was to please all his fans and admirers with his
farm scenes, and farmers who knew sheep appreciated
that here was an artist who knew the Downland
breeds, Leicester, Herdwick and Blackface. Those who
bred pigs saw that he knew Saddlebacks and
Tamworths. When it came to farm machinery…
Tunnicliffe went to the implement makers…*

above
John Piper
*East Barsham Manor,
Norfolk*, 1981

top
John Piper
*Royal Arms at Thame
County Court* from
the *Shell Guide to
Oxfordshire*, 1953

John Piper

There's a very up-market art gallery in the little Rutland town of Uppingham where, if you stare at the pictures for long enough, a pretty girl will ask you if you'd like a cup of coffee. But I am now running the risk of a) being asked to pay rent or b) being mistaken for a grisly exhibit because I spend so much time in there just staring open-mouthed at the Pipers.

Here is a painter, illustrator and designer whose passion for buildings and landscape literally glows out of his pictures. Very often the backgrounds will be dark and sombre (hence King George VI's comment about Piper being unlucky with the weather) with inky blues and greeny blacks, but invariably church towers and country houses shine out in ghostly but brilliant hues. Some pictures, like his magnificent painting of Harlaxton Manor in Linconshire, look like they're etched in ethereal lines of neon light. And in and out of it all are careful and knowledgeable depictions of architectural details, many of them gleaned and appreciated through his long association with friend John Betjeman and their tours of English counties for the Shell Guides.

John Piper holds a very special fascination for me because he championed, as did Betjeman, the forgotten and neglected.

left
John Piper
Seaton, Rutland, 1978

above
John Piper
*Harlaxton Manor,
Lincolnshire*, 1977

Through both his writing and photographs
I learnt to love what he called 'pleasing decay',
his epithet for the concept that not everything
has be pristine and well ordered to be innately
beautiful. The enlightened thought that the
weather is just as an important contributor to
the look of an old building as an architect's
plan. Lichen and moss ruling OK.

S.R. Badmin

opposite
S.R. Badmin
Matlock, detail from a
watercolour reproduced
as a magazine give-away

above left
S.R. Badmin
Title page drawing from
*The Ladybird Book of
Trees,* 1963

above centre
S.R. Badmin
Illustration of elms from
*The Ladybird Book of
Trees,* 1963

above right
S.R. Badmin
September from *The
Shell Guide to Trees and
Shrubs,* 1958

Badmin crops up all over the place. I paid homage in *Unmitigated England* to his contribution to *Radio Times* front covers and his work for Shell, and elsewhere in this book to his remarkable efforts on behalf of Puffin Picture Books. But any study of the depiction of the English landscape in the last eighty years or so would be missing the point if it didn't include his meticulous portrayals of rural life and scenery.

Stanley Roy Badmin was born on 18 April 1906 in the South-East London suburb of Sydenham. After winning a scholarship to Camberwell Art School and a studentship to the Royal College of Art he was elected an Associate of the Royal Watercolour Society in 1932. As the 1930s drew to their ominous pre-war close he completed his stunning illustrations for *Highways and Byways in Essex* for Macmillan and *Village and Town* for Noel Carrington at Puffin. The Second World War saw Badmin working for the astonishing 'Recording Britain' project, the Pilgrim Trust's frantic quest to illustrate buildings and places that, it was feared, would succumb to destruction by the Luftwaffe.

Anybody looking at Badmin's work at this time would have been left in no doubt as to his unique skill in rendering the trees in his landscapes. (Anyone who loves his work can't look at a stand of chestnuts around a pantiled farmstead without saying, 'Very Badmin.') Post-war editors queued up to commission him for a variety of books – *British Countryside in Colour* for Odhams, *Famous Trees* by Richard St Barbe Baker, the *Shell Guide to Trees and Shrubs* and, the iconic *Ladybird Book of Trees* in 1963. But Badmin was most often found out there painting his immaculate watercolours, paintings that offer any number of different 'walks for the eye' and heart-warming discoveries of the minutiae of life – foxes eluding huntsmen on snowy downs, lovers closing gates on recently-shorn cornfields, villagers gossiping over stone walls. And of course the trees, always the trees. Churchyard elms, landmark firs, orchard blossom. Serried hillside rankings, bare riverside skeletons; all seasons, all weathers.

Rigby Graham

above
Rigby Graham
Stoke Dry, Slurry Slave,
1997

below
Rigby Graham
Clitheroe Cement Works,
1997

Most people arriving in Stoke Dry will make a beeline for the tiny church perched on the side of the Eye Brook Valley. Easels and tripods set up to capture the sixteenth-century porch or the perfect grouping of rectory, church and farmhouses. But not Rigby Graham. Oh no, he tips up in Stoke Dry and immediately spies a discarded slurry tank gradually sinking into a grass verge, the cow parsley growing up around the axle, counterpointing electric poles and cables. And so, off he goes, hunched up against the weather, applying his thick waxy Russian watercolours to record a Rutland scene that I think is just as typical of the county as lonely church towers and ironstone manor houses. In Malcolm Yorke's fittingly titled biography *Against the Grain* Graham sums it up: 'Things which are harmonious and completely resolved I want no part of. Anything in equilibrium is static.'

Rigby Graham's career of painting and printmaking is extraordinarily prolific. Born in Stretford in Lancashire in 1931 he perhaps acclimatised himself to a lifetime of sitting about outside by landing at Rosslare at two o'clock in the morning on 1 January 1948, walking in the snow to Dublin, sleeping rough,

above

Rigby Graham
*Broughton Castle
Gatehouse, Oxfordshire*,
1992

right

Rigby Graham
*Castle Bolton, North
Yorkshire*, 1997

and then doing it all in reverse. For much of his life Graham taught in colleges and schools in Leicester, but in latter years the walls of Mike Goldmark's gallery in Uppingham have seen a literally brilliant succession of paintings of the surrounding countryside, the paint still looking wet as if from a recent shower. John Piper wrote in 1986: 'I have known Rigby Graham and have admired his work for a good many years. He has an unusual and indeed enviable capacity to make romantic and dramatic images out of simple scenes – sometimes almost totally deserted ones…' I wonder if Piper was ever tempted by a slurry tank in the rain.

above
Simon Palmer
Cycling Home, 1996

opposite
Simon Palmer
*The Lost Portrait of
Penelope Plain*

right
Simon Palmer
*Meeting at the Meridian
Canal Summit*

Simon Palmer

You can recognise an evocative link weaving like a gentle breeze through the tall trees of Simon Palmer's paintings to end up on Paul Nash's doorstep. Melting February snow on furrowed fields, the slightly eerie juxtaposition of shadowed ball-finialled gateposts with pale moons. Mr Palmer is at one with his particular patch of country, North Yorkshire. Agricultural as opposed to moorland; corrugated iron and collapsed metal gates as opposed to bucolic lyricism. But this is not nostalgia for a lost world, this is another world altogether.

The quality of the watercolour rendering of natural subjects stands up there with the very best of English landscape painting, but here there is something else. Not afraid to detail his pictures with road signs and bus stops, Simon Palmer also peoples them with mysterious figures flitting amongst the trees and undergrowth. An Icarus flaps frantically in the distance over pantiled farm buildings, tall-hatted strangers warn of roadside nymphs, sinister figures wait by tunnel ventilators. Questions never answered; left to us to work our way through the painter's imagination or, better still, for us to make something up with our own. What goes on in the Meridian Canal Summit watchtower? Why does Penelope pose in the shadows of the hedge?

ENGLISH LETTERS

If a society cares about trivialities such as saving or creating a fine piece of lettering, it will probably care about the building it is on, and care about the street that it's in, and care about the town the street is in, and care about the country itself...
Fascia Lettering, Alan Bartrum

opposite
Fat woodcut letters, particularly in variants of Egyptian typefaces, were favourites for big Victorian signs and posters

My first job (almost) was in a commercial art studio above a post office in Leicester. I was allowed in as a junior, and in between refilling water jars and emptying waste bins – I had to carry the collected rubbish down to the street and heave it into the back of the dustcart myself whilst my superiors chucked balls of screwed-up paper at me from the upstairs windows – I took my first faltering steps in learning how to draw lettering. My first test was to paint, using a ruling pen, the *Vogue* magazine logo, which was stuck down under a piece of blue plastic film called Kodatrace. If you made a mistake you corrected it with a tiny blade that scraped the errors off the film. I took five hours to do this and when I proudly took it to the studio manager he lifted up the film and all the letters fell out on the floor.

It was the inauspicious start to six years' hard labour and a love / hate relationship with alphabets. But once I'd cracked it I learnt to love lettering in all its forms, even when I in turn was looked at blankly by designers in my care, who turned away from my 'When I was a boy the pencil was still on the secret list... ' lectures to stare at their Apple Macs.

As soon as I'd saved £15 for a rusting Ford Thames van I was off on my English tours, and one of the richest pleasures was discovering good examples of the lettercutter's or signwriter's art. Shop fascias, the numbers on locomotive tenders (never written down, honest), gravestones, stallholders' chalked price tags for cauliflowers and carrots. Incisions into slate, brushstrokes on brickwork, gold leaf on glass, vitreous enamel on iron.

We need to look out for, and appreciate, good lettering with a fresh eye. We live in a time when we are swamped by words, so much so that they run a great risk of being devalued and rendered illegible. Think about appalling graffiti logos hailed as *the* new art by those who should know better. Think about your local roundabout with its shrubs and bark chippings, now sponsored by your local accountant, with a miserable sign tapped out one lunch hour on a computer. Good lettering is the suit of clothes that brings wording on signs to life, and used with thought and care it can help us to stop drifting remorselessly into a depressing homogeneity.

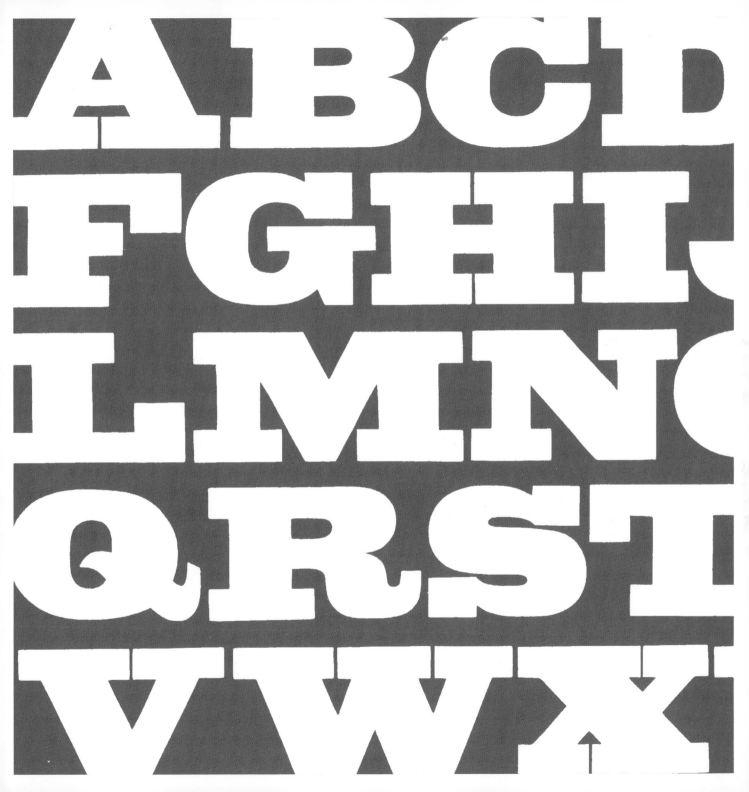

IN MEMORY OF
.LTER BERNARD BENT
ELDEST SON OF
ENRY AND MARY BENT
OF HAWLEY LODGE
OCT 26TH 1904

.nemory ..
.MAS MULLINGTO
.O DIED JAN II 1850

memory

Ann

William

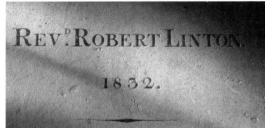

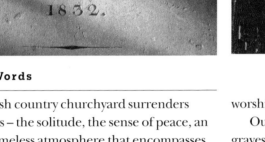

Grave Words

opposite, clockwise from top left
Brookwood, Surrey;
Owston, Leicestershire;
Great Tew, Oxfordshire

above left
Fotheringhay,
Northamptonshire

above right
Churchyard notice,
Fosdyke, Lincolnshire

below
Yardley Hastings,
Northamptonshire

An English country churchyard surrenders many joys – the solitude, the sense of peace, an almost timeless atmosphere that encompasses all we deeply feel about the continuity of life (even though we are surrounded by the last resting places of those who would most likely have sung praises in the church now standing guard over them). If the churchyard is not too carefully manicured then there is the additional pleasure of nature elbowing its way in with long pale grasses and butterflies flitting amidst the stone and slate. Even in the cool of the church itself we can see memorials on the walls or in the floors, constant reminders of those who worshipped here over hundreds of years.

Our eyes will be continually drawn to the gravestones; the leaning markers that tell simple family stories in deeply cut incisions. They not only give us epitaphs of life and death; they can also impart art lessons about the styles of lettercutters and carvers. There will be regional differences of material, the variance of local fashions and continual experimentation with the new alphabets arriving in the latest editions of printers' type books.

It is very rare to find a tombstone dated before 1600, and the best are undoubtedly those erected in the eighteenth and nineteenth centuries, before the machine age took over, with names, dates and sentiments spaced out in stock letters mechanically let into the highly polished slabs of marble. The most stunning of the earlier markers are unquestionably those fashioned from large pieces of slate – impressive monuments that could easily have been positioned the week before, the only real clue to their age (apart from the dates) being the angle of lean as the soil has shifted and changed around them.

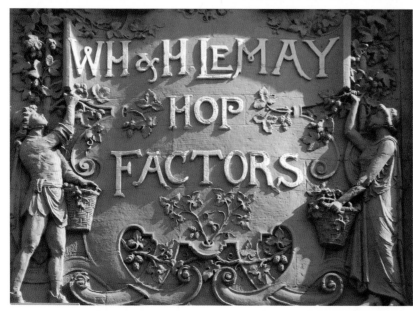

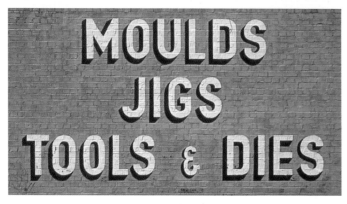

Writing on the Wall

Applying lettering up on gable ends and high above eye level on buildings has resulted in some remarkable survivors. For years I passed a sign up on a wall in the Old Kent Road that advertised London's 'First Flickerless Cinema', but sadly it appears to have finally been obliterated.

Here is a wall of a building out in remote Lincolnshire that is amongst the best I've seen, and even though dealing in flour and cake is no longer a priority, the lettering is still kept up to scratch. An extinct workplace reminding a village of its past. But who in York still takes 'Nightly Bile Beans'? LeMay's Hop Factors terra-cotta cartouche still chimes with the Kentish hop fields reached from nearby London Bridge station and the Birmingham factory wall could easily be the life story of an overalled Brummie in a machine shop.

below left
Factory wall in the
Jewellery Quarter,
Birmingham

centre left
Borough High Street,
London

above left
Gable end in York

above right
Bath house in Stamford,
Lincolnshire

opposite
Gable end in Bardney,
Lincolnshire

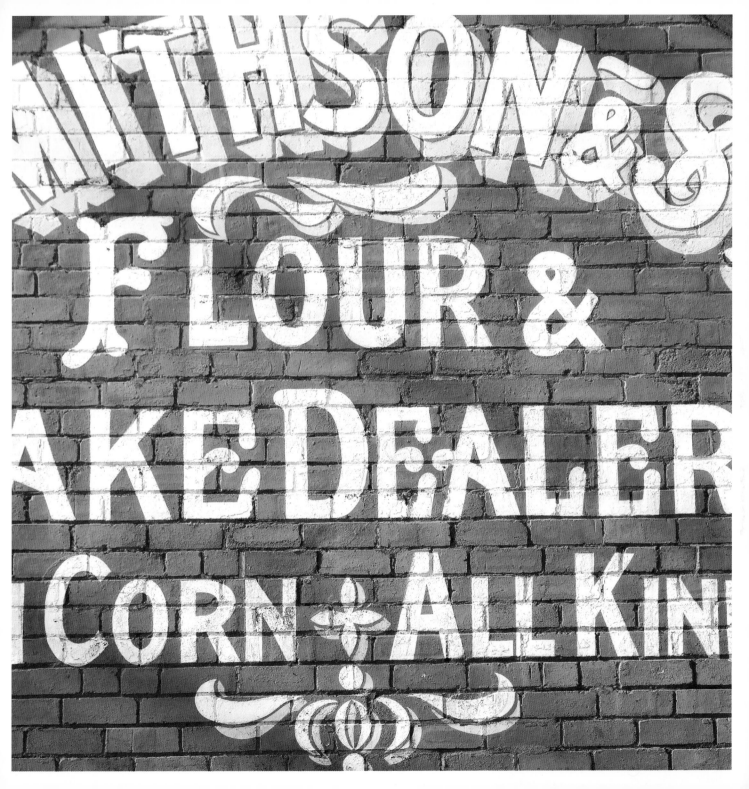

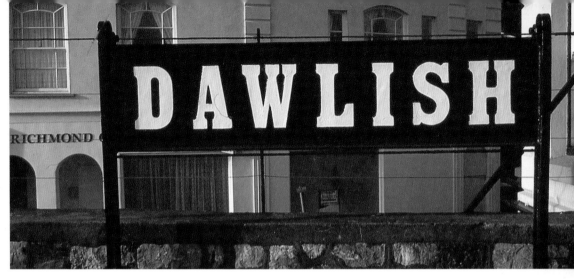

Railway ABC

There was once such an air of confidence and singularity of purpose about railways that all their communications were of the very highest standards in terms of design. Except of course it wasn't design at all, just an in-built sense of producing signs and messages in an uncluttered and unambiguous style. A draughtsman would draw up a nameplate for a locomotive, as naturally as he would plan a buffer beam; a typesetter would proof a 'fragile' label for the parcels office without having to look up the relevant section in the corporate identity manual.

Everything from station signs to tickets had an air of permanence about it. Built-to-last iron signs with vitreous enamel legends, metal typefaces imprinted into thick cardboard. Signwriters' deft brush strokes guided paint over traced lines to put shadowed numbers onto steam locomotive tenders and railway crests onto carriages, blacksmiths' hammers forged cut-out speed limit signs. A station timetable was a masterpiece of the typographer's art, a sticker on a carriage window telling you a compartment was for 'Ladies Only' would probably be set with wood type. Even the oversized names on wooden-planked wagons and steel tankers looked right (surprisingly), the train moving through the countryside as a sequence of mobile posters. But no laptops here, no conference calls to decide where the packet of sausages should go on a Palethorpes truck.

Above all, there was once an innate honesty. Everything one looked at said, 'We are a railway.

above left
Cast-iron speed limit sign

above right
GWR station sign,
Dawlish, Devon

**below right and centre
and opposite, bottom right**
LNER labels for the
transit of livestock, glass
and ladies

below left
'Dora' is a locomotive that
steams up and down the
Nene Valley Railway in
Cambridgeshire

above
Station sign in
Adlestrop's bus shelter,
Gloucestershire, with the
platform seat

top left
Ceramic lettering at
Exeter St David's station,
Devon

top right
Wagon side at Didcot,
Oxfordshire

You are our passengers. We will do our best to get you to your destination without patronising you with meaningless jargon into thinking you're travelling with easyJet.' But even in these days of the relentless money-grab of changing franchises and the red-hot microwaved sausage in a flaccid bun, there are still hints of a much more satisfying past to be seen through the hermetically sealed coach windows. I do hope Dawlish is still defying the corporate manual with its original GWR (Great Western Railway) station sign in glorious Egyptian capitals, and that the chocolate-coloured ceramic hand still points to other platforms at Exeter St David's.

One sign I know is safe: the original sign for the vanished Adlestrop station, now in the village bus shelter. Here is the name recalled by Edward Thomas in his eponymous poem:

Yes, I remember Adlestrop –
The name, because one afternoon
Of heat the express-train drew up there
Unwontedly. It was late June.

Moving Letters

above left
Foden fairground truck
cab

above right
Fellows, Morton &
Clayton canal boat
lettering at the Ellesmere
Port Boat Museum,
Cheshire

below
An ice cream van once
seen in and around
Coventry

There is a rich and lively tradition of painting anything that moves. Amongst the first vehicles to find lettering on their sides must have been the express stagecoaches, which took full advantage of the newly improved roads of the late eighteenth and early nineteenth centuries. Red and black mail coaches with Royal ciphers and names like Highflyer, Comet and Rocket. The railways continued the tradition by lettering their fire-snorting locomotives in embossed brass – Leviathan, Thunderer, Vulcan. Canal boats were superbly signed. In the boatyards they called it 'ticking-in' – big-shadowed letters in primary colours ablaze amidst the rushes and blue brick locks.

The advent of the internal combustion engine soon saw commercial bodies fitted to the chassis designed for motorcars, ideal canvases for signing up the ownership of lorries and vans, buses and coaches. These early days saw the continuance of a lettering tradition that manifested itself as a peculiarly English popular art, now all but vanished except on traditional fairground rides. Egyptian and Clarendon typefaces, which shared a common heritage with theatre posters printed in wood type, and beautifully cursive scripts that echoed the copperplate of business cards.

The page opposite demonstrates the rarefied heights to which van owners were encouraged to rise in the late 1930s. Commercial art indeed, and vans painted like this really did appear on England's roads. It is rare to see a decently signwritten van nowadays. Most vans are delivered in white; most of the lettering is equally as imaginative. Any tradition is fast disappearing. It was once sustained very successfully by that ubiquitous highway carrier, Eddie Stobart; the dark green vehicles lettered in an emphatic yellow and red. That is until it was apparently decided that this instantly recognisable livery was simply not cutting-edge enough to reflect 'global aspirations' or whatever. So in came the designers, out came the laptops and everything we liked about Eddie's lorries disappeared at the click of a mouse. It was like somebody decanting Lyle's Golden Syrup out of that glorious tin and into tupperware.

opposite
Illustrations from a
c. 1935 brochure for
Morris 10 and 5 cwt light
vans, demonstrating a
wide range of liveries.
I want to drive around
delivering butter in the
Meadow Dairy van

Yarmouth, Isle of Wight

Bedford

Whatstandwell, Derbyshire

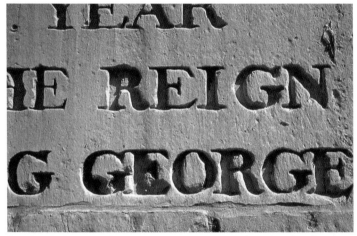

Obelisk, St George's Circus, Lambeth

Stamford, Lincolnshire

Hallaton, Leicestershire

Somerdale, Keynsham, Bristol

Dungeness, Kent

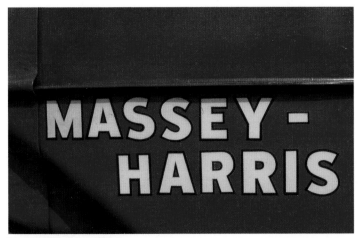

Tractor, Wrotham, Kent

Torquay, Devon

Ludham, Norfolk

Oundle, Northamptonshire

Services Rendered

opposite
Hydrant sign for the deftly-named Market Harborough and Little Bowden Water Works, once serving this Leicestershire town

above left
Fire hydrant plate in Chipping Campden, Gloucestershire

above centre
Electricity service plate in Orme Court, Bayswater, London

above right
Service indicator on the verge outside Yaldham Manor in Kent

below
Coalhole in Park Square East, Regent's Park, London

For those with a nose for interesting signs, it's always worthwhile looking underfoot, rummaging about on grass verges and staring at otherwise blank walls. Here we can find the long lost service providers, still pointing the way to hydrants in the road and things lurking underneath pavements. I wonder when the Market Harborough and Little Bowden Water Works last sent water gushing through the mains? I imagine it was around the same time as the big, no-nonsense indicator pictured opposite was still looked out for by brass-helmeted firemen. And I bet in those days the MHLBWW looked after their water too, and didn't go on about putting breezeblocks in your lavatory cistern and insisting you share a bath with your neighbour.

The yellow painted fire hydrant sign still strikes a happy note in Chipping Campden. I love the heavy Bodoni letters and the fact that it still uses proper measurements to do its job. Perfect for this Cotswold town; perfect for anywhere really. But sometimes something

more substantial is needed. The stone indicator for Mid Kent Water sprouts forth from wayside herbage outside Yaldham Manor in Kent, the letters sporting a distinctly flared-trousered look. Hopefully the bright brass Metesco badge can still be founded imbedded into a London service hatch, constantly buffed by the soles of Bayswater on a pavement in Orme Court.

What looks like a manhole cover here is in fact a cast-iron coalhole. You'll find them in Regency and Victorian streets where the coal cellars are underneath the pavements, reached from the basement yards of the houses. They meant that coal could be delivered without disturbing the household, or perhaps more specifically they curbed the enthusiasms of Ned the coalman for Polly the scullery maid. Either way, the lettering still tells of a vanished foundry, and Sampson's was very local to this particular coalhole.

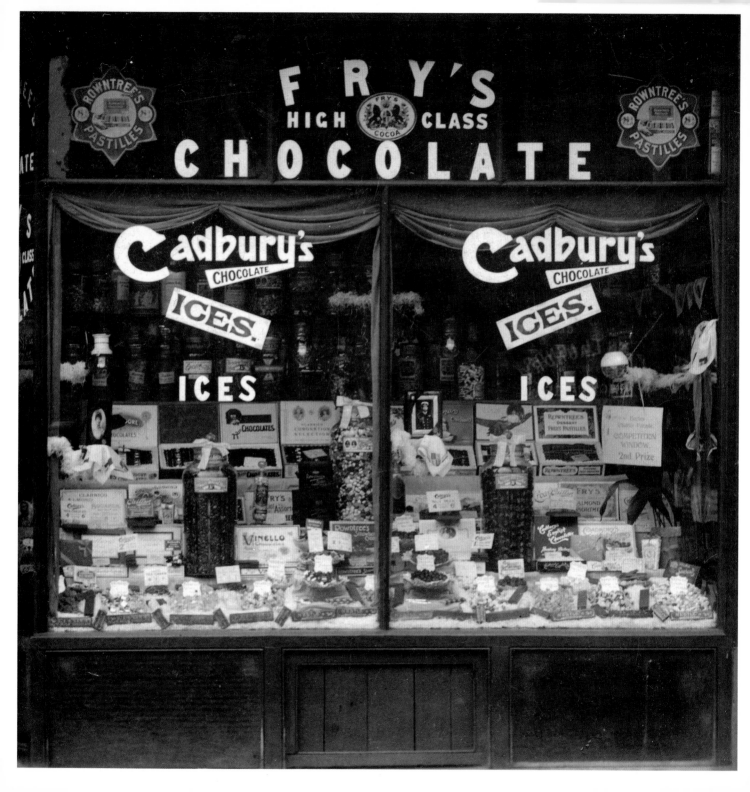

Shop Talk

opposite
Polly and Arthur
McAlpine's sweet shop
near Manchester, *c.* 1910

above left
More writing on the wall
in Bridport, Dorset

above right
A disappearance in
Stow-on-the-Wold,
Gloucestershire –
Woodward's shoe shop

below
A bountiful flowing script
from a baker's paper bag

Lettering proliferates in the retail environment. Alphabets are marshalled into line to communicate countless messages to customers, from the smallest line of type on a packet of tea, through paper bags to fascia panels above shop windows. Sadly, all too often these messages are the bland stereotypes of the chain store; identikit plastic panels run out across the nation in the smallest number of common sizes. With no respect for the integrity of the buildings, England's high streets lose any notion of local character. Even at this level individual shops can suffer from signs that betray the fact that the trickiest part of the exercise has been booting up the computer.

Thankfully there are enlightened retailers of all sizes who recognise that their street credibility is only enhanced by giving thought to signing, which extends beyond just backlighting the corporate logo, and actually consider the local style of building.

At one time a signwriter would have subconsciously taken these factors into account, with most typestyles being drawn from paint-spattered alphabet books or from a customer's notepaper. Even mass-production achieved a certain sensitivity, seen here in Cadbury's thin white cut-out metal letters applied to glass. Genuine crafts, now all but lost, as any number of variants can be run out from a computer file.

GREEN · DRAGON · HOTEL ·
CATERING FOR LARGE & SMALL PARTIES
ACCOMMODATION FOR MOTORISTS & CYCLISTS
GOOD STABLING & MOTOR PIT ·
McMULLEN & SON
WINE

Assorted Alphabets

Once you start looking, interesting lettering talks to us from a host of unlikely places. The 1903 Green Dragon Hotel in Hertford is sadly no more, but the terra-cotta and gilt lettering lives on. 'Good Stabling & Motor Pit' has echoes of the ghosts of phaetons being overtaken on the Great North Road by be-goggled motorists in Panhards and Napiers, but the name McMullen still lives on as an independent brewer that once had a brewery in Hertford town centre. Even Niklaus Pevsner noted this characterful wall in his Buildings of England, *Hertfordshire.*

A bookshop chain has taken over Joseph Emberton's 1935 Simpson's building on Piccadilly, but the personality of the former clothes store is still to be seen in the simple Art-Deco lettering at pavement level. Lettering also survives, surprisingly, in the entrances to shops and public houses. Long lost names still trodden underfoot as customers push open doors. (In Dartmouth there's still a Hepworth's.) In Leicestershire the Coach & Horses in Anstey retains its name in the doorway, the beautifully decorative mosaic redolent of an almost Roman extravagance. And on the waterfront in Hull the ladies'

opposite
A stunning terra-cotta wall in Hertford, Hertfordshire

this page, clockwise from top left
Simpson's Art-Deco shop sign in Piccadilly, London; a public house entrance in Anstey, Leicestershire; floral carving for a public convenience in Hull, East Yorkshire; a neon sign in Notting Hill Gate, West London

lavatory is announced in a graceful cartouche – how much better than an anodised metal plate with a bland silhouette of a woman in a rah-rah skirt stamped on it. But why do I get a slight frisson of male anxiety when I see this neon window sign in Notting Hill Gate?

above
Wooden letter 'J' for large posters. The actual size is 16 inches deep

above right
Yorkshire Post newsstand poster, set in wood type for just one day in 1959

opposite
A selection of a Norwich printer's wood type. The blank bars at the bottom are spacers, the equivalent of the leading for metal type

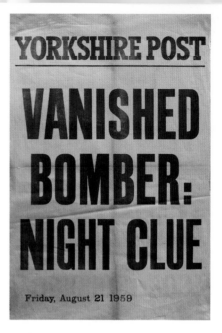

Wood Face

In 1970 I ended up working for a Leicester printer, who happened to be just about the country's largest purveyor of metal type to other printers all over the country. The idea was that for half the time I would design things, for the other half I would travel the queen's realm dispensing the type. Until one fateful afternoon when I slammed on the brakes of my Hillman Husky and I was showered with about 45,000 pieces of 8 point Baskerville, which I had failed to secure properly. Two seconds before the tractor pulled out in front of me they had been the galleys of a carefully set book on its way to a printer in Coventry. It took me a week to hoover it out of the car and about an hour for my future prospects to come under critical review.

None of this dampened my enthusiasm for type, but I must confess I felt more at ease with the big wooden letters that didn't hold such potential for disaster. By the 1970s they were becoming obsolete of course, only really used for big simple display posters and newsvendors' dramatic headline notices. And then one day a designer I knew, who worked for a printer in Norwich, was sitting with his feet up on his desk, idly watching workmen trundling wheelbarrows across the yard and tipping their contents onto a roaring bonfire. Intrigued, after half an hour

he went out and, in true designer style, had a pink fit as he saw them burning acres of wooden type. The destruction was halted and he filled his car up with the survivors, later giving me a couple of boxfuls.

What messages did they shout out, what exhortations in coloured inks did they exclaim? Presumably, looking at the samples opposite, nothing much with the letter Q in it, but just look at the capital R, rosy red from countless inkings. Each one is a beautiful object in its own right, their textures and patina of colours now mutely telling of a long life being pressed up against sheets of paper. I wonder how many pieces ended up on designers' kitchen walls or imbedded into glass-topped coffee tables, how many hours were spent trying to spell out rude words backwards. But I hope there's someone, somewhere, in a green apron and smoking a Capstan, still inking them up and proofing them, just because it must be such a very satisfying thing to do.

opposite, clockwise
from top left
Beach life in Hastings,
East Sussex; Dartmoor,
South Devon; *Through the
Looking Glass* lettering
revealed when a red
brick Wesleyan chapel
was demolished on the
Fens; vitreous enamel
sign at Quainton Road
station, Buckinghamshire
Railway Centre; street life
in Hastings

this page, clockwise
from top left
Eleventh Commandment
in a country churchyard,
Kirk Ella, East Riding of
Yorkshire; emphatic cast-
iron street signs in Louth,
Lincolnshire; Southern
Railway carriage class
and something I can't
really explain, an impulse
purchase of a Maidstone
& District bus destination
blind

BOOKS AND STUFF

One book above all others should now be on the book-shelves of the enthusiast and explorer of *Unmitigated England*. If you're as bonkers as I am about books you may want to invest in two copies. One for the shelf, one with the cover taken off to use constantly like a well thumbed AA Handbook, if they still existed:

England in Particular Sue Clifford & Angela King (Hodder & Stoughton 2006)

A Good Book and a Mug of Cocoa

For the children's books obsessive, the series of Collector's Books by Eric Quayle is invaluable, sadly now out of print. And the prices quoted are obviously out of date. The most entertaining and beautiful book on the subject that I have found is:

Children's Book Covers Alan Powers (Mitchell Beazley 2003)

Books on individual series of titles are starting to appear as collecting mania grips the bibliophile by the dust jacket. A classic example is the little book cataloguing Observer's Books, produced as a facsimile of one of the later editions:

The Observer's Book of Observer's Books Peter Marren and John Carter (Peregrine Books 1999)

William Companion Mary Cadogan (Macmillan 1990)

For more about Edward Ardizzone, Judy Taylor has got together a collection of the illustrations with which the artist liberally peppered his letters:

Edward Ardizzone: Sketches for Friends Chosen and Introduced by Judy Taylor (John Murray 2000)

Favourite books can easily be picked up on the Internet, but I would always recommend rummaging about in second-hand bookshops, and particularly at book fairs. Cocoa's a bit more difficult. Cadbury's still make it (more as a cake ingredient perhaps than a comfort beverage), and when I trawled online to look for suppliers I got the Care Of China's Orphaned and Abandoned Children, which is probably a much more worthwhile thing to find out about.

How to Watch Cricket

The bible is of course *Wisden*, a little but fat volume in a yellow jacket that makes an annual appearance. A friend has built up a collection of every edition since the year he was born; that's how cricket gets to those who know more about it than I do. With a bit of luck you may be able to get the two books I mention with their John Gorham covers, but any edition will do:

The Penguin Cricketer's Companion Edited by Alan Ross (Penguin 1981). The first edition was published by Eyre & Spottiswoode (1960), and a revised and expanded second edition was issued in 1979.

The Village Cricket Match John Parker (Penguin 1978)

The incredible variety of cricket pavilions is admirably shown in only one book that I know of:

The Pavilion Book of Pavilions Jonathan Rice, photographs by Paul Barker (Pavilion 1991). I wonder how long it took them to come up with the title?

The Marylebone Cricket Club (MCC) is the centre of the cricket universe. To get in your father has to put your name down when you are born, and even then you have to wait seventy years until someone dies. But try wearing their 'egg-and-tomato' tie at Lord's when you're not a member and you'll get frog-marched off to the Long Room where the committee chairman will do something to you with a cricket stump. But the MCC also does an essential, and very cheap, book of rules:

The Laws of Cricket (MCC 2003)

A Post Box Collection

Books on the subject of post boxes are rare; it is, after all, a fairly obscure subject unless you're a philatelist whose interest extends beyond stamp albums and those fiddly little mounts. But here are a few worth taking a look at:

The Letter Box Jean Young Farrugia (Centaur Press 1969)

Pillar Boxes Jonathan Glancey (Chatto & Windus 1989)

I-Spy In the Street (News Chronicle Publications *c.* 1955)

Pillar to Post Henry Aaron (Frederick Warne 1982)

There is also The British Postal Museum & Archive, which has a store of stuff hidden away in Essex somewhere, where they occasionally open the doors so you can take a quick peak inside.

Englishmen's Castles

Books about ordinary homes and houses are as various and numerous as different front doors. Here is just a small alcove shelf full:

The Castles on the Ground J.M. Richards, cover by John Piper (The Architectural Press 1946). There are later, much less expensive editions.

Houses for Moderate Means Randal Phillips (Country Life 1936)

Villages of Vision Gillian Darley (Paladin Books 1978)

Palaces for the People Greg Stevenson (Batsford 2003)

Little Palaces (Middlesex University Press 2003)

The 1930s Home Greg Stevenson (Shire 2003)

Letchworth: The First Garden City Mervyn Miller (Phillimore 1989)

Trumpet at a Distant Gate Tim Mowl and Brian Earnshaw (Waterstones 1985)

I would be failing in my duty if I let my natural modesty stand in the way of giving a big plug for a book I produced with Philip Wilkinson, which, amongst many other building types, puts houses in their chronological and historical context:

The English Buildings Book Philip Wilkinson and Peter Ashley (English Heritage 2006). And now in an equally large paperback.

The Ghosts of Christmas Past

There is not a huge bibliography of books just about Christmas by individual authors, not forgetting Charles Dickens of course. There are lovely editions of his Christmas books produced by Pears Soap between the wars, which include *A Christmas Carol*. Most appear to be anthologies, but one of the most enjoyable is still my Christmas Eve companion:

The Christmas Book Enid Blyton (Macmillan 1944)

The Twelve Days of Christmas Miles & John Hadfield (Cassell 1961)

Christmas: Penhaligon's Scented Treasury of Verse and Prose (Pavilion 1989.) This book comes in a red slipcase, and might still retain a hint of the Christmassy scent they introduced to the pages during production. Chocolate Orange? Stilton?

Roll Out the Barrel

Don't read books about beer and breweries unless you're doing a thesis or something similar. Just get out there and drink a few pints or hang about outside the brewery of your choice, sniffing the air before loading the back of the car up with stock. Most regional breweries will have a shop that will sell sample cases of individual bottles and, of course, barrels to get racked up in the kitchen, or in your cellar if you're lucky enough to have one. But if you've been chained to your armchair, sample these books by CAMRA (Campaign for Real Ale):

Dictionary of Beer Edited by Anne Webb (CAMRA Books 2001)

The Big Book of Beer Adrian Tierney-Jones (CAMRA Books 2005)

And one that is really irresistible, just for the title alone:

Brewery Breaks: Great Days Out At Over 100 Real Ale Breweries Ted Bruning (CAMRA Books 1997)

Sunlight on the Meccano

When Robert Opie was sixteen he was about to throw away a Munchies wrapper when the thought occurred to him that nobody was recording or seriously collecting packaging. After years of his subsequently gargantuan collection weighing down the floors of a Gloucester warehouse, and then being shunted out by Dev the Developer, The Museum of Brands Packaging and Advertising finally found a good home in Colville Mews in London's Notting Hill. A much more worthy day-out than trying to find Hugh Grant's front door from the eponymous film. Opie has also edited a superb series of scrapbooks; brilliant montages of brands, packaging and ephemera from all eras from the Victorian to the 1970s. Other enlightening books:

How Household Names Began Maurice E. Baren (Michael O'Mara Books 1997)

How it All Began in the Pantry Maurice E. Baren (Michael O'Mara Books 2000)

Down the Cut

Naturally the very best thing to do about seeing the canals is to take a holiday on a narrow boat, or even just a day-out. Or take a good long walk down a towpath. Canal literature covers every single aspect you could possibly want to know about, and a good deal you could probably do without. There are also highly detailed maps and more decorative canalware than you could ever find a use for. I got very excited by it all when I produced a little book, *Grand unions*

(Everyman Pocket Books / English Heritage 2002), but I was very aware that I was trespassing in an area of interest that was peopled with profound experts, much as one finds if you get too involved in railways. Have a dip into the following books and you will be able to bluff your way through a conversation with a bargee or boatyard engineer:

Narrow Boat L.T.C. Rolt (Eyre & Spottiswoode 1944; Sutton Publishing 1994)

The Inland Waterways of England L.T.C. Rolt (George Allen & Unwin 1950)

The Canals of England Eric de Maré (The Architectural Press 1950)

Canals Nigel Crowe (Batsford and English Heritage 1994)

Umbrellas and Paint

Paintings and associated images are best seen 'in the flesh' as it were. You'll find Eric Ravilious's work in a number of galleries, certainly in the Towner Gallery in his home town of Eastbourne. Edward Bawden was a benefactor of the The Fry Gallery in Saffron Walden, and they have over one hundred and fifty pieces of his work in their collection. Chris Beetles knows all about Mr Badmin and usually has a few drawers full of his work in his Mayfair emporium, but for John Piper and Rigby Graham you need look no further than the Goldmark Gallery in Uppingham. The last time I poked my nose round the door I was confronted by Ravilious lithographs and had to run away. Simon Palmer can be found at JHW Fine Art, London.

There isn't the space to detail all the many books on the artists I have talked about, but here's a shot at a basic list:

The British Landscape 1820–1950 Ian Jeffrey (Thames and Hudson 1984)

Paul Nash David Boyd Haycock (Tate Publishing 2002)

John Nash: The Delighted Eye Allen Freer (Scolar Press 1993)

Eric Ravilious: Imagined Realities Alan Powers (Philip Wilson / Imperial War Museum 2003)

Edward Bawden Douglas Percy Bliss (Pendomer Press 1979)

Design: Edward Bawden and Eric Ravilious Brian Webb & Peyton Skipwith (Antique Collectors' Club 2005)

Tunnicliffe's Countryside Ian Niall (Clive Holloway Books 1983)

Piper's Places Richard Ingrams and John Piper (Chatto & Windus / The Hogarth Press 1983)

S.R. Badmin and the English Landscape Chris Beetles (Collins 1985). A rare and stunning book conceived and put together by The Albion Press.

Simon Palmer (Various catalogues, JHW Fine Art)

English Letters

We don't see type books very often these days, if at all. They were once the staple of the printer's office or the commercial art studio, traced off at different sizes for typographic layouts, blown up to large sizes on mysterious fridge-like objects called Grant Projectors. Now, everything from narrow columns of type to huge architectural signage starts life in a computer programme. Sometimes great care is taken with the result; more often it's not. To see just how characterfully the letter styles of the past have enriched our environment, there are some important and stimulating references:

Signs in Action James Sutton (Studio Vista / Reinhold 1965)

The English Lettering Tradition Alan Bartrum (Lund Humphries 1986)

Signwritten Art A.L. Lewery (David & Charles 1989)

Designage Arnold Schwartzman (Chronicle Books 1998)

There is also a lovely little series of paperbacks on lettering collected and commentated upon by Alan Bartrum: *Street Name Lettering*, *Fascia Lettering*, and *Tombstone Lettering*, all published by Lund Humphries in 1978.

ACKNOWLEDGEMENTS

My grateful thanks to Jonathan Meades for his insightful preface.

Misha Anikst, Ben Ashley, George Ashley, Kathy Ashley, Wilfred Ashley, Lucy Bland, Simon Bland, David Campbell, Kathleen Cherry, Peter Creese, Rupert Farnsworth, Mike Goldmark, Richard and Jane Gregory, Emma Hibbert at Adnams, Leigh Hooper, James Huntington-Whiteley, Alfonso Iacurci, Clémence Jacquinet, Ian Joules, Stuart Kendall, Sarah Peacock, Biff Raven-Hill, Margaret Shepherd, David Stanhope, Tony Unsworth, Christina Usher, Carl and Helen Warner, Philip Wilkinson.

I am also indebted to my aunt, the late Helen Newton, for the use I made of the scrapbook she put together for my cousins in the 1940s and '50s.

Images

Unless otherwise noted, the images in this book are from the author's personal collections. For the images on the following pages the author and publisher would like to credit:

pp. 22–23: All pictures © Estate of Edward Ardizzone.
p.91 (bottom left): © The Royal College of Art.
p.98 (top & centre): Reproduced by kind permission of Adnams.
p.55 (top right): © Andrew Davidson. Courtesy of the Artworks, London.
pp.125 & 146 (top right): © Canal+ UK Image Ltd.
p.127 (top right): © George Mackley.
pp.140 & 154–55: All pictures reproduced by kind permission of the Goldmark Gallery, copyright Rigby Graham.
pp.142 & 143 (top right): Reproduced by kind permission of The John Nash Estate/The Bridgeman Art Library.
p.143 (top left & bottom): © Paul Nash Trust
pp.144 (top) & 145 (top): © Estate of Eric Ravilious/DACS 2007. Reproduced by kind permission of Mrs Anne Ullman.
pp. 150–51: All pictures © Estate of John Piper.
pp.152–53: All pictures courtesy of Chris Beetles Gallery, St James's, London.
pp. 156–57: All pictures reproduced by kind permission of JHW Fineart.

Text

For permission to reprint the following copyright material the author and publisher gratefully acknowledge:

p.14: Extract from 'Leisure' by W.H. Davies. Reprinted by kind permission of The Literary Trustees of Walter de la Mare and The Society of Authors as their representative.
p.94: Extract from 'Christmas' by John Betjeman © The Estate of John Betjeman.
p.106: Extract from 'Middlesex' by John Betjeman © The Estate of John Betjeman.
p.154: Extract by John Piper from a letter written in 1986, published in *Rigby Graham at the Goldmark Gallery*, published by Goldmark (1987). Reproduced by kind permission.
p.155: Extract from *Against the Grain* by Malcolm Yorke, to be published by Goldmark (late 2007). Reproduced by kind permission.

Every reasonable effort has been made to contact copyright holders of material reproduced in this book. Any omissions are entirely unintentional and should be notified to the publisher, who would be glad to hear from them and will ensure corrections are included in any reprints.

INDEX

The author wearing his Patent Discriminator Goggles, which successfully filter out the harsher realities of life.

Photograph: David Stanhope